THE
NEW
AMERICAN
HIGH
SCHOOL

CORWIN
PRESS

The Corwin Press logo—a raven striding across an open book—represents the happy union of courage and learning. We are a professional-level publisher of books and journals for K–12 educators, and we are committed to creating and providing resources that embody these qualities. Corwin's motto is "Success for All Learners."

THE NEW AMERICAN HIGH SCHOOL

David D. Marsh
Judy B. Codding
and Associates

CORWIN PRESS, INC.
A Sage Publications Company
Thousand Oaks, California

For information:

Corwin Press, Inc.
A Sage Publications Company
2455 Teller Road
Thousand Oaks, California 91320
E-mail: order@corwinpress.com

SAGE Publications Ltd.
6 Bonhill Street
London EC2A 4PU
United Kingdom

SAGE Publications India Pvt. Ltd.
M-32 Market
Greater Kailash I
New Delhi 110 048 India

Printed in the United States of America

Library of Congress Cataloging-in-Publication Data

The new American high school / edited by David D. Marsh, Judy B. Codding.
    p. cm.
    Includes bibliographical references and index.
    ISBN 0-8039-6225-8 (cloth: acid-free paper)
    ISBN 0-8039-6226-6 (pbk.: acid-free paper)
    1. High schools—United States. 2. Educational change—United States. 3. Education, Secondary—United States—Administration. 4. Education, Secondary—United States—Curricula.   I. Marsh, David D. II. Codding, Judy B., 1944–
    LA222.N49 1998
    373.73—ddc21
    98-9079

This book is printed on acid-free paper.

01 02 03 04 05 7 6 5 4

Contents

Foreword

Lauren B. Resnick
University of Pittsburgh

WE HAVE COME full circle. Here is a book, written as we prepare for a new century, that echoes some essential aspects of recommendations made by a distinguished group of educators and public citizens more than a century ago. In 1893, the Committee of Ten, a group of leaders from some of America's most prestigious educational institutions, debated how the American high school should adapt to the growing demand for secondary schooling. The standard high school program of the day featured a "liberal arts" curriculum with mathematics, languages, history, and geography at its core, and, although only a small minority of students went on to college, the schools served as preparatory institutions for higher education. It was evident that few of the new secondary school attendees were likely to pursue a college education or enter the professions. The committee nevertheless concluded that a liberal education, focused on cultivating the mind, would be valuable for everyone regardless of the path they might follow later.

The Committee of Ten's ambitious vision did not prevail. The committee had argued against "vocational education"—using schools to train young people for specific jobs. But vocationalism and "adaptation to life" in fact became the order of the day as American secondary education expanded. The view that came to dominate was that the high schools should directly prepare young people for the kinds of postschooling life they were most likely to lead. This view accorded well with the social theories of the time: that society and individual students would be best served through early identification of young people's "natural talents." Students who would not be able to benefit from a rigorous intellectual education, it was argued, would be spared the discomfort of such demands. At the same time, society would benefit from having well-trained workers for its growing factories and other industrial jobs.

From this theory and its incorporation into an efficiency-oriented model of school management, there emerged in the succeeding decades a differentiated public secondary schooling system. Separate programs for college preparatory, technical, and commercial programs developed. As enrollments expanded, especially during the Depression years of the 1930s, many non-college preparatory students could not be accommodated in commercial and technical programs, some of which had become sophisticated, challenging, and expensive to run. As a result, a "general program," neither technical nor college preparatory, emerged. Most children of working-class families tended to be enrolled in this general program that led nowhere in particular.

Except in a few large cities, Americans have preferred comprehensive high schools to separate schools for different types of programs. The popularity of comprehensive schools has been based on a belief that bringing all of a community's young people together in a single secondary school will better prepare them for a democratic life together. Within the comprehensive school, however, the technical, commercial, general, and college preparatory programs have largely functioned as separate tracks, with minimal opportunity for shared educational experience. Theoretically, students could take individual courses from any program, but they rarely explored outside their own, and guidance counselors often discouraged such experiments. Although a high school's extracurricular program was in theory meant for all students, in practice, students from the different tracks segregated themselves (or were guided by faculty) into separate activities. Many communities managed to draw all their high school students into a single building, but the students received radically different educational opportunities once there.

David D. Marsh and Judy B. Codding and the other authors of this volume want to undo the tracking system entirely and return, in an updated sense, to the Committee of Ten's vision. They argue for a high school with only one purpose: to provide a high-quality academic education for all students. Focused on core subjects such as mathematics, science, and English, the new American high school would expect everyone to work toward a common, high-standard academic credential (the Certificate of Initial Mastery, or CIM). Differentiated programs would be delayed until after the core credential was earned. The high school itself would offer continued college preparation—at a level consonant with today's Advanced Placement or International Baccalaureate programs. Technical and career programs would be offered by other educational institutions, sometimes in collaboration with employers who would provide supervised internship opportunities to qualified students.

Although the core vision of a vigorous academic program for all students is similar to that espoused by the Committee of Ten, much of what is proposed here represents a significant departure from current practice in American high schools. Perhaps most fundamental is that age-grading in the high school would end. The common academic program would be standardized in terms of the kinds and quality of learning demanded. But it would be flexible with respect to how long it might take to earn the CIM. Some students might earn it at 15 years of age, many at age 16; and significant numbers, at least at the outset, might not earn it until age 18 or even later. Differences among students would be accommodated not by lowering expectations but by varying the time accorded to core studies.

A second key difference from older proposals for a high school liberal arts core is the focus on outcome standards. The authors outline a standards-driven high school program with criteria for high-quality performance that are explicit and internalized by students and teachers alike. Descriptive scenarios of standards-based classrooms and schools bring the vision to life. These are not just dreams for the future. They are scenarios drawn from the real experiences of the authors as teachers, principals, and other leading educators. Theirs are voices of the real and the possible.

This does not mean that the job will be easy. Indeed, the courageous educators who take the lead in creating standards-based high schools will need unusual degrees of perseverance, dedication, and flexibility. Why should such an apparently simple idea—creating clear expectations for academic achievement and making a credential contingent on meeting those expectations—be so challenging? The answer lies in the way we have allowed time spent in school to take on a value unrelated to what is actually learned while there. In the decades since the advent of the comprehensive high school, America has created the illusion of greater education by keeping more young people in school longer. But our population today is not really better educated, despite the dramatic increase over the years of the proportion of students who complete high school.

The problem we face today is that merely setting standards and enforcing them through a credentialing process would reveal the lie that we have been living. Many students who have come to view completing high school as their right would now fail. To establish standards and not simultaneously organize to teach all students well cannot be an acceptable social policy. It would break the implicit social contract that has promised young people that staying in school will be rewarded with a credential, the high school diploma, valued by society.

This book outlines a plan that goes beyond setting standards. It is a plan for organizing high schools and secondary school teaching so that every student has a real chance to learn what the standards ask of him or her. It is a plan for teaching everyone seriously and well— children of the poor, minorities, immigrants and English learners, as well as students from the more privileged families. A plan such as this is, I believe, a moral imperative for those who espouse higher standards of learning.

This may be the right historical moment for the kind of high school reorganization called for in this volume. Throughout the 20th century the high school has been the public institution responsible for managing and facilitating young people's transitions from childhood to adulthood. The high school has served as both capstone of schooling for children and entryway to the workplace. Only a minority, increasing over the decades, has continued in an educational institution beyond the high school years; for most young people, high school was the point of articulation from childhood to being "in the world." For growing numbers of Americans, college is now this articulation point. The proportion for whom this is so is likely to grow rapidly over the coming decade. A national sense of entitlement to higher education is being created through enlarged loans and grants and by a public rhetoric promising that no one will be denied a college education for financial reasons. Proposals for secondary education programs that might restrict eventual college attendance for graduates encounter resistance from families and from the general public. This shift, both rhetorical and real, toward higher education as the gateway to adult status and opportunities creates both demand and opportunity for radically redefining the high school. A high school whose main function is college preparation makes more sense today than it did 50 years ago.

Getting the college story straight is essential to understanding the meaning of what is proposed in this book. When Americans speak of college or higher education opportunities for everyone, they often do so without explicitly considering our very diversified higher education system. For some, college means a selective 4-year institution—public or private—with a liberal arts orientation. For many others, it is a 4-year institution with an essentially vocational (or "professional") undergraduate program. By 1990, over half of earned baccalaureate degrees in the United States were in professional fields, including business, health-related professions, engineering, recreation, and law enforcement. For yet other young people, college means a community college, with either a clearly technical orientation or a loose relationship to the 4-year institutions.

All these varied institutions are called "colleges." All are routes into adult roles. But they provide very different educational experiences. What they have in common is the requirement of a basic academic preparation. That is what the CIM is meant to provide. After that, there are multiple ways of entering college: further preparation in the high school for the more selective liberal arts programs (including some college-level work in the high school itself); direct entry into less selective 4-year or 2-year programs; or joining a career program that combines community college or technical institute training with some form of internship experience.

This book looks to a future in which the majority of Americans will go on to some form of college. It envisions a high school that can return to its original purpose of shaping the minds of young people and that seeks to do so for all young people rather than a select few. In terms appropriate for today, with due appreciation of the variety of students our high schools must teach, it reaffirms what the Committee of Ten proposed over a century ago:

> Every subject which is taught in a secondary school shall be taught in the same way and to the same extent to every pupil so long as he pursues it, no matter what the probable destination of the pupil may be, or at what point his education is to cease.

The time may have come when this radical idea can become a reality.

Preface

FOR ALMOST 50 years, the comprehensive American high school has been a familiar and comforting feature of the American landscape. For most of us, it has marked the end of childhood and the scene of our rites of passage to adulthood. The high school years could have been the time we met our future wife or husband, the time we first found out we were really interested in cars or physics, the time we got our first real job, the time we first realized that we were going to leave the home that we grew up in, with all the hopes and fears that entails, or the time we went out for varsity sports and first heard the intoxicating roar of the crowd in our ears. For most of us, high school is when we first really began to find out who we are and think about what we might become.

One reason that this institution has been so many things to so many people is because it was designed that way. The people who shaped it were convinced that only a few American students were capable of serious academic study and would go on to the kind of work that would require serious academic preparation. For the rest, high school should be a place to grow up, to acquire the practical skills they would need as homemakers or tradespeople, to learn about the habits of personal health, safety, and home financial management that they would need as responsible citizens and parents, and, not least, to acquire the values of effort and honor and the will to win that competitive sports provides. From the woodworking shop to the chemistry labs, from the football field to the chorus, there was something for everyone.

When we tucked our yearbook under our arm at the end of our senior year, though, we knew who would go on to be a store clerk and who would go on to be a university professor. We knew because, although the high school was comprehensive, it was by no means uniform. A great deal was expected academically of a few, and very little was expected of many. There was never much doubt about who was who. Comprehensive it might be, but egalitarian it was not. The comprehensive American high school is like an ocean. On the surface, it all looks like water, but in fact strong currents flow through it and hardly mix at all. This is very like the high school, with its own social groups, each in its own place in the social system of the school, each pinned to its position in the hierarchy of what is expected academically.

We who contributed to this book do not agree on every detail of our vision for the American high school. But we are in agreement that it is time to abolish the comprehensive American high school. It is time to recognize that there is less of a future every day for the graduate who is not a fluent reader, who is not a competent writer, who does not know that light can be equally well described as a wave motion in an electromagnetic field and as a stream of discrete photons, and whose facility with mathematics stops at arithmetic.

The fundamental premise of the comprehensive high school, that only a few need to graduate with solid academic accomplishments to their credit, no longer holds. The American high school must now be reconceived and redesigned with one goal in mind: to make sure that every graduate has the academic skills and knowledge needed for entry-level college work. Not that everyone needs to go right to college right after high school. But all need to be ready for it, without remediation, immediately. That is the task.

Few if any American high schools now meet that challenge. This book is about what it will take for any high school to reach that goal.

The fulcrum of this book is the idea of the Certificate of Initial Mastery (CIM), first proposed by the Commission on the Skills of the American Workforce (1990) in its landmark report *America's Choice: high skills or low wages!* Imagine a standard of academic performance for high school students based on what is expected of most 16-year-old students in core subjects in nations where performance is highest. Imagine that a certificate is given to every student who meets that standard. Imagine that the highest priority of every high school is to make sure that all but the most severely handicapped students meet that standard before graduating. That is the idea of the CIM. It represents a commitment to getting every student to a clear, hard standard of academic excellence. It is that simple and that daunting.

Another way of describing what this book is about is to say that it is about what it will take to give virtually all our students a certificate like that—how the American high school will have to change to make that possible, and what else the high school can do when it achieves that goal to advance the academic preparation of our students for demanding college programs.

Judy Codding and Robert Rothman begin in Chapter 1, "Just Passing Through: The Life of an American High School," by capturing the challenge in the most vivid way possible, through a portrait of a typical high school in a typical midwestern town. The town is located in a state where academic performance has been consistently high over the years and is itself relatively free of the kind of racial strife and extreme poverty that account for very low student performance in our big cities. And yet . . . and yet the picture that emerges is one of utter failure of the school to do its job, to graduate students who have the skills and knowledge they need to succeed. Rothman and Codding analyze this failure, and in doing so, present a detailed, unvarnished picture of the real nature of the challenge our high schools face.

There are no villains in this chapter. Everyone involved is a person of goodwill. Most are doing their best as they see it. This makes the failure all the more painful. But it is precisely this quality, this sense that this might be any town, that it is not very different from many towns, that makes this story so pertinent as the starting point for the subsequent chapters.

In Chapter 2, "How Did We Get Here, and Where Should We Be Going?" Marc Tucker helps put the hard reality of the school just seen into a perspective fashioned in part from the development of the American high school over the decades and in part from an appreciation of the ways the evolving national economy has changed the context in which the current American high school operates. We begin to see why the high school described by Rothman and Codding met the needs of the 1950s very well, but does not meet the needs of the end of this century. Tucker describes the origins of the idea of the CIM and shows how a CIM could be constructed by states or districts and how it would operate. He introduces the idea that the whole lower division of the high school should be focused on getting every student to the CIM, whereas the upper division should be focused on a demanding college prep program for the students who have their CIM and are going on to a 4-year college. Finally, he introduces the idea that many students who get their CIM will not want to go right on to a 4-year college, but will need a new kind of professional and technical program, usually including some college that gets them ready for a rewarding career. This framework, in which the CIM serves as fulcrum, sets the stage for the rest of the book.

The CIM, of course, is of no value unless the standards on which it is based are clear and there is an accurate way to measure student progress toward those standards. In Chapter 3, "Standards and Assessment: The Foundation of High Student Achievement," Robert Rothman describes the kind of performance standards that are needed in detail, distinguishing them from content standards. Using the New Standards™ system as an example, Rothman shows how student portfolios can be constructed that use end-of-course examinations, reference examinations, and other assessments to build a record of student accomplishment referenced to the standards.

In Chapter 4, "Rethinking Curriculum and Instruction in the New American High School," David Marsh and Philip Daro describe the principles for constructing a high school curriculum matched to the standards. They emphasize the importance of focusing each course on very few topics, each of which is really understood by the student before he or she progresses to the next course, and the need to stress conceptual mastery of the material as well as the ability to apply what one is learning to real-world problems. The chapter describes extended lessons as the essential building blocks of curriculum, and stresses the importance of carefully designing these extended lessons to build up the student's capacity to handle the material.

Sally Hampton, in Chapter 5, "Standards-Based Classrooms in High Schools: An Illustration," describes what a classroom in the new, standards-based American high school would look like. She describes what we would find on the wall, how students would use the standards as they go about their daily work, how teachers would refer to the standards in their conversations with students and use them in evaluating their students' work. We leave this chapter with a three-dimensional, engaging image of the texture of everyday life in the standards-based high school classroom.

In Chapter 6, "Beyond the CIM: Pathways to the Future," Jacqueline Kraemer, John Porter, and Marc Tucker describe in some detail what the program should be for students who have received their CIM. They lay out a program for students who want to stay in high school to prepare themselves for examinations to get into competitive 4-year colleges. Then they describe another program for students who, after they get their CIM, want to participate in a combination of classroom work in school and college and work-based learning, all leading toward an occupational certificate that qualifies them for jobs leading to rewarding careers. These professional and technical programs would typically include work in community or technical colleges and would in most cases result in the student receiving a 2-year college degree.

Judy Codding and Marc Tucker pull all the pieces together in Chapter 7, "A New High School Design Focused on Student Performance," to describe a design for the new American high school, a design intended to get every student to the CIM standards, using the standards, assessments, curriculum, instructional systems, and post-CIM components described in the preceding chapters. They show how new accountability systems, approaches to professional development, planning systems, master schedules, and ways of involving everyone in the enterprise can be joined together to create a new kind of high school. This is a design for a high school focused exclusively on results, with no excuses for failure, a high school whose standards are at least as high as the standards for Scarsdale and Beverly Hills high schools but a high school for everyone, not just the elite.

We then turn from the high school itself to a description by David Marsh and Mike Strembitsky in Chapter 8, "District Redesign: Direction, Support, and Accountability for Standards-Based High Schools," of the things that have to change in the way that the school district is organized and managed to make possible the kinds of changes we have described taking place in high schools. The focus here is on the need for the district to define the standards the students will be trying to reach; to make it clear which professionals will be held accountable in which ways for which aspects of student performance; to provide support to the high school in appropriate areas and to provide clear direction in those areas in which direction is appropriate; and to distinguish between direction on the one hand and support on the other.

The book concludes, in Chapter 9, "Some Tough Choices Ahead," with a synthesis written by David Marsh, including a summary of the key elements needed for student success in a standards-driven high school, as well as some of the choices one will have to make if, in fact, a school will act on the belief that all of its students can and will achieve at high levels.

Acknowledgments

WE HAVE BEEN on a long journey trying to rethink high school education in the United States. In this, we have learned both from our own work in high schools and from the many colleagues who have strengthened our ideas and perspective. They have made this book possible. We would especially like to thank Marc Tucker, president of the National Center on Education and the Economy, whose ideas, wisdom, and leadership have significantly influenced American education and our work. His insight about policy, practice, and program development opened important doors for all America's children and youth. He has truly been an inspiration and mentor.

Recently, we worked with the National Center on Education and the Economy (NCEE) and its related subdivisions, New Standards and the National Alliance for Restructuring Education. Both of us deeply admire many of our colleagues in those organizations. We would like to thank Harold Asturias, Merle Audette, Cynthia Betances, Ann Borthwick, Phil Daro, Sally Hampton, Patricia Harvey, Sally Mentor Hay, Loretta Johnson, Tom Jones, Jackie Kraemer, Mary Anne Mays, David Mintz, John Porter, Bob Rothman, Marge Sable, Elizabeth Stage, and Mike Strembitsky for being truly wonderful colleagues. Lauren Resnick's command of the research literature and her wise counsel have been great assets in our work.

We would especially like to thank the current superintendent of the Pasadena Unified School District, Vera Vignes, for her wisdom and strong support. John Porter in the district office was essential in creating important academies at Pasadena High School. Within the school were many dedicated teachers who made this all possible, especially two assistant principals, Kathy Leslie and Fred Zimmerman. Students, teachers, the community, and family partners, as well as these school and district leaders, taught us that all students can learn and that schools can be reformed—even if the lessons are, at times, painful.

We would also like to thank long-term colleagues, including Sherry King, the late Larry Kohlberg, Debbie Meier, Fred Newmann, and Ted Sizer for important conversations and collaborative thinking about what high school could and should be. But our colleagueship has extended beyond the borders of the United States. Each summer at the University of Southern California (USC), David Marsh codirects the International Principals Institute with Brian Caldwell from the University of Melbourne, Tom Jones from the National Center on Education and the Economy, and Brent Davies from the University of Lincoln in England. Looking at school leadership from an international perspective has taught us many lessons that guide our work, as do unique contributions from England, Australia, and the United States that have made practical and real our hopes and dreams.

At USC, colleagues such as Gib Hentschkle, Ed Lawler, Allan Odden, Larry Picus, and Penny Wohlstetter have extended our thinking about school reform and school leadership. We owe them a real debt of gratitude. We'd also like to thank wonderful graduate students Isabelle Bespalko, Juli Quinn, and Suzanne Tacheny for their work in helping to implement these changes in schools, as well as providing research and editing support for the book itself. Todd Sahara, an administrative assistant at USC, has been invaluable managing the office and managing the production of this book. We also would like to thank Alice Foster at Corwin Press for her extensive insight about schools and important counsel about the shape of this book.

To Suzie Sullivan, we express our gratitude for all her support.

Finally, we would like to thank our families for their support and involvement. David would especially like to thank his father, who was one of the finest school principals in the land, as well as Maryalice and Myranda for their professional and personal counsel and support.

Judy would like to thank her husband, Richard, and her children, Barbara, Amanda, and Richard, for their support and encouragement during her many busy years as a high school teacher and principal.

About the Authors

Judy B. Codding is vice president for programs at the National Center on Education and the Economy. A former teacher at the elementary, middle, and high school levels, Codding has also been an award-winning principal of one of Los Angeles' toughest high schools as well as of some of the wealthiest schools in New York's Westchester county. She was one of four charter principals who participated in the creation of Theodore Sizer's Coalition of Essential Schools. She is co-author with Marc Tucker of *Standards for Our Schools: How to Set Them, Measure Them, and Reach Them.*

Philip Daro is Executive Director of New Standards and the Director of Research and Development for the National Center on Education and the Economy. New Standards is a collaborative effort involving 17 states and 6 school districts, the purpose of which is to create a national assessment system for the nation's schools. His career has included tenure as Director of the Office of Project Development with the California Department of Education, Executive Director of the American Mathematics Project, and Executive Director of the California Mathematics Project.

Sally Hampton is perhaps best known for her work in education reform within the areas of English language arts and applied learning. Her current work focuses on developing assessments that support the rigorous curriculum required for students to meet higher standards. Since 1991, she has been involved with New Standards as both a site coordinator and a consultant in its assessment efforts, including its innovative work with portfolios of student work. In 1995, she was asked to develop frameworks for a set of performance standards, and subsequently the reference examinations that would tie to those frameworks. She is Director of Research on Curriculum and Instruction and English Language Arts for the National Center on Education and the Economy.

Jacqueline Kraemer is Senior Associate with the Workforce Development Program at the National Center on Education and the Economy. She works on state workforce development policy and has done research on international skill standards and training systems. Before joining the Workforce Development Program, she worked on child and family policy with the Harvard Family Research Project, directed operations for a community school program in West Philadelphia, and researched youth apprenticeship for the International Labor Organization.

David D. Marsh is a Professor of Curriculum and Instruction at the University of Southern California and Director of the USC Center for School Leadership and Transformation. He is a coauthor for the California task force report *Second to None*, and recently completed studies of middle school reform, the role of state curriculum frameworks in school improvement, and the enhancement of principals as instructional leaders. He was recently appointed as the Robert A. Naslund Professor of Curriculum Theory, the only distinguished chair professorship in the USC School of Education. Three years ago, he received a Fulbright Scholarship in India, where he worked for 3 months with the Central Ministry of Education on improving high schools.

John Porter is Director of New Sites and School to Careers at the National Center on Education and the Economy. He has taught high school and served as a high school principal and superintendent of schools. He created a series of school designs that emphasize aca-

demic and vocational integration, tech-prep, and youth apprenticeships, among them Project ALIVE. At the National Center on Education and the Economy, he is a national consultant and presenter and
a school-to-career consultant to several state and city jurisdictions. He
has studied on-site the workforce investment and educational systems in Denmark, England, and Scotland.

Robert Rothman is the author of *Measuring Up: Standards, Assessment,
and School Reform* (1995), an analysis of the shift in standards and
performance assessment. Formerly Associate Editor of *Education
Week*, and Director of Special Projects at the National Center on
Education and the Economy, he is currently Program Officer, Board
on Testing and Assessment at the National Research Council.

Michael Strembitsky is Senior Fellow of High Performance at the
National Center on Education and the Economy. He served as the
superintendent of schools in the Edmonton Public Schools (Alberta,
Canada) for 22 years. As superintendent, he focused on improving
student achievement and stakeholder satisfaction. Prior to becoming
superintendent he taught at all precollege levels and held numerous
administrative positions. He has served as a consultant to many
school districts in the United States and Canada; as Chairman of the
Board of Directors, Agency for Instructional Technology; Chairman of
the Large City Superintendents, Canada and the United States; and
President of the Canadian City Superintendents. Among his awards
is the Province of Alberta Achievement Award for Education.

Marc S. Tucker is President of the National Center on Education and
the Economy, a nonprofit organization engaged in policy analysis and
development, institutional design, and technical assistance in education and human resources. He created the National Alliance for Restructuring Education, the Commission on the Skills of the American
Workforce, New Standards, with Lauren Resnick, and the National
Board for Professional Teaching Standards, with Governor James
Hunt. Together with Ray Marshall, he wrote *Thinking for a Living:
Education and the Wealth of Nations,* winner of the Sidney Hillman Prize
for 1992, and with Judy Codding he wrote *Standards for Our Schools:
How to Set Them, Measure Them, and Reach Them.*

Part I

*Where We Are and
Where We Ought to Be*

1

Just Passing Through
The Life of an
American High School

Judy B. Codding
Robert Rothman

BY ALL ACCOUNTS, the second half of the 1980s was one of the most energetic periods in American history for education reform. In state after state, governors, legislatures, and boards of education adopted sweeping policies to strengthen course requirements, upgrade the teaching force, and much else. Dozens of commissions issued voluminous reports calling for reform in teaching, curriculum, and assessments. Foundations and government agencies poured millions of dollars into new textbooks, new tests, and new teacher education programs.

All this activity produced some significant changes. The proportion of high school students taking a challenging academic program nearly quadrupled between 1982 and 1994. Student achievement in mathematics and science increased significantly, and the gap in performance between white and minority students shrunk. And, despite fears that the reforms would drive students out of school, the high school graduation rate and the number of students taking the SAT have both increased—as have scores on the test.

3

Yet, despite these improvements, there is substantial evidence that high schools have in fact changed little since the early 1980s. The gains brought about by the reforms represent, at best, half a loaf. Although the number of students enrolled in an academic course sequence rose sharply, half of high school students still have not taken such a program. The gains in science and mathematics performance are not matched in reading: Reading performance remained relatively flat during the 1980s and 1990s. Even in science and mathematics, the improved performance is still far from exemplary as the 1998 Third International Mathematics and Science Study (TIMSS) of 12th-grade students points out; students in the U.S. lag behind peers from other nations in international comparisons of math and science achievement. The performance gap is not limited to our weaker students. Only the top 5% of students in the U.S. score better than the average Japanese student on international tests of mathematics performance (U.S. Department of Education, 1996).

The state of student performance reflects a stubborn and unfortunate truth: The teaching and learning in many American high schools, and the way the schools are organized and structured, remains just as it was when the reform period began. This is not because many schools have been immune to the reform fever; on the contrary, one would be hard-pressed to find a high school not engaged in some kind of reform. But these reforms have not transformed the schools in any significant way. Reforming teachers remain oases within the school, which carries on as it did for years; reforming schools remain islands within the larger system.

Consider the following description, from a 1985 book. It is as valid today as it was when it was written:

> Most students and teachers are satisfied with the education available from their own high schools. People can work as much or as little as they wish. Students who do little work can still pass in return for orderly attendance; students and families who want more engagement and push for it can usually get it. . . . Teenagers designated by some group tend to receive special attention. . . . Those who are average or unspecial are usually left alone. They use high schools as they choose, without pressure from either the school or an external lobby. Complaints are few. "Why should we?" they say. "We just want to get out." (Powell, Farrar, & Cohen, 1985, pp. 4-5)

There is one major difference between 1985, when *The Shopping Mall High School* (Powell et al.) was written, and 1998. Now, the consequences for the "unspecial" are, if anything, more serious than they were a decade ago. Now it is much more difficult for those who just get by to secure a productive future. The failure to engage a large proportion of American youth and to provide them with the education they need to live fulfilling lives in the next century will prove harmful—to the nation as well as to the young people themselves. For that reason, the prevailing practice in high schools needs to change.

What is the prevailing practice? With more than 15,000 high schools in an incredibly diverse nation, this question seems difficult to answer, but in fact it is quite easy—distressingly so. One of the authors served as a high school principal in one of the most affluent areas of the nation, as well as in one of the poorest, and both of us have visited and studied schools in a wide range of settings. The same characteristics crop up again and again. We see schools with a multitude of purposes, unable to focus on what really matters—student achievement. We see little attention to performance data and an inability to plan by using information. We see students, regardless of background or aspirations, who would rather be almost anywhere else but in school, yet who remain simply to get their tickets punched and get on with their lives. We see teachers who measure their success by the extent to which they can cover the textbook, not by how much students learn. Above all, we see a system that does not see its purpose as ensuring that all students achieve at high levels.

These conditions prevail even in the most advantaged, high-achieving schools. These schools contain unspecial students, just as most high schools do. They get lost in the shuffle while the school devotes its attention, and earns its reputation, from the top students. The difference in the high-achieving schools is that students there have parents who actively support their children's education and drive them to succeed academically, whereas schools serving more disadvantaged students often lack this. As a result, advantaged students work hard and do well in school—in many cases, despite the conditions of the school itself.

In small towns and inner cities, these problems pose real risks for the children who attend the high schools. In these places, students just pass through high school. The undemanding curriculum, the lack of any kind of personal attention, and the lack of a commitment to ensure the best opportunities for every student pose real harm to the future lives of the students who manage to graduate, not to mention what happens to those who do not see their way to a diploma.

To get an idea of these kinds of high schools in the 1990s, the kind of institution that needs to change if schools are to educate all students to high levels, we visited a school in the middle of the country. Though no school is really typical—all schools are unique in some way, reflecting the population and culture of the place—the description of this school should ring familiar to anyone who has been in a high school recently. Educators all know students and teachers like the ones in this place, and they have seen practices very much like those that go on here.

On the surface, the school is very much like the kind of high school one might see on television or in the movies. Located in a small city in the midwest, it has a nearly all white, working-class student body. Although it has a reputation as a "tough" school, it is clean and orderly.

Beneath the surface, this school shares many of the features that put it squarely in the national mainstream—troubled waters indeed. Student achievement is low, and although the teachers and administrators want to do something about it, there is a pervasive sense that there is little they can do. Teaching methods, with a few exceptions, remain the same as they have been for generations. Some students do well, whereas large numbers of students leave without the knowledge and skills they need to become productive citizens.

This school opens a window into the troubling condition of high schools in the United States at the close of the 20th century. It also illustrates the challenges reformers face in reshaping the system so that all students achieve at high levels.

GW: High School in the Heartland

The train tracks that cut through the parking lot and divide the two main buildings of George Washington (GW) High School serve as a vivid symbol of the city in which the school is located and the students who attend it. This was a railroad town, at the intersection of a number of major rail lines; until the early 1970s, when trucks overtook trains as the major mode of interstate shipping, the railroads were the town's major industry.

As the presence of the tracks indicates, GW retains a blue-collar character. The school is located in a part of town dotted with small factories and a grain elevator, and the prefabricated bungalows in the area suggest a much more modest level of income than the larger single-family dwellings in the hills to the east. Ask residents about GW, and they will tell you that, of the three high schools in the city, it is the one where the "troubled" youths go.

The inside of the school belies that reputation. A new building, which houses the athletics programs and music rooms, is spotless, and the older building, originally built in 1922, is nearly as clean. Students—allowing for the usual adolescent restlessness—are generally orderly. Students generally walk, not run, down hallways, and the between-class din is kept to a dull roar.

Lunch periods are a little more hectic, but not much. In place of a lunchroom, GW has a lunch cart in a corridor, where students order inexpensive fast food. Even here, decorum prevails. Students form a line that snakes through the corridor, and the teenagers and adults respect the order of the line. The school's orderliness is enforced by a uniformed police officer, brought on campus 4 years ago in the wake of evidence of gang activity. But the police officer is not a dominating presence. Students, parents, and teachers all say that people care about the school and keep it safe.

The school's reputation for toughness probably stems from the economic background of the student body. Half of the school's 1,300 students qualify for free or reduced-price lunches, although only about 20% actually receive the subsidized meals (many students eat lunch off campus). Many students, if they graduate from high school, will be the first in their family to do so. About half the graduating class goes on to some form of postsecondary education—half to 4-year colleges and universities and half to community colleges—and most of the rest go into the armed services or directly to work. Some, young women, particularly, stay home after high school and start families.

The GW community is an unusually close one. Because people who grow up in the town tend to stay there, many of the parents of current students themselves attended the school. So have many teachers: As much as a third of the GW faculty are alumni. Yet although this close kinship means that teachers, parents, and students share a common bond, it does not mean that teachers see their primary role as one of ensuring that all students perform at high levels academically. The teachers tend to believe that some students will make it and most will not, and even though they may like the students as individuals, they do not think there is much they can do to change what they see as the facts of life.

The school ties of parents and faculty may also reinforce a sense of traditionalism in the school. Parents and teachers want the school to remain the way it was when they attended. As one science teacher, who attended a different high school in the same city, put it,

> I would say education in the U.S. is pretty much the same as it has been for as long as I've been in it. As a student and educator, that's 25 years. I don't see a lot of difference. I see a difference in technology, of course. But the way education is approached is not a lot different. I see myself doing the same things I had done to me when I was a student.

Thus, the organization and practice of the school remain fairly conventional. The school has a 7-period day, with 50-minute periods. In nearly every classroom, students sit in rows facing the teacher's desk; the only exceptions are an honors English class, where students sit in semicircles, and computer rooms, where students sit at the computer workstations around the periphery of the room. The course offerings are varied, though not as extensive as in some schools. The course descriptions make up 10 pages in the student handbook and include a range of vocational and business courses as well as English, mathematics, science, history, and foreign languages.

Some time ago, in a formal curriculum plan, these courses had important content connections and a coherent sequence. But these links have mostly been lost, and teachers at GW now have only a vague awareness of how the courses actually fit together. Teachers point to their own creations—the courses, each unique in design and style, that they teach. But students know the truth. They know that the assignments, terms, and techniques that last year's teachers thought were so important are nearly invisible in their classrooms this year. Next year another course will be experienced, completed, and soon forgotten.

The method of instruction is rather conventional as well. For the most part, instruction is teacher directed and textbook driven. Coverage of chapters in the textbook defines the goal for most teachers at the school, despite the recent emphasis in the research literature about the importance of curriculum depth. Moreover, there is little opportunity for students to find anything authentic in their learning, to generate their own problems, or to connect their work to the world outside of school. To get a flavor of the kind of instruction that typifies the GW approach, walk into an algebra class on a Friday morning. For the first half of the period, the students go over homework problems they worked on the night before—a strategy that builds little understanding of the big ideas or the solution strategies to the specific problems. The problems require students to apply a formula for solving quadratic equations, the subject of the current unit. The many exercises are variations on a theme; in each, students plug in different numbers and manipulate the equations until they get them into standard form. Only one problem appears different from the rest: The numbers are considerably larger. After solving the problem, the teacher notes, parenthetically, that the equation just solved is the equation that describes the Gateway Arch in St. Louis. The students seem unimpressed by this isolated fact.

During the discussion, the students ask the teacher to work through problems they have trouble with. The teacher goes through the steps on the blackboard, occasionally asking students to suggest the next step. The teacher actively discourages students from trying approaches that vary from the textbook method. At one point, one student offers a suggestion that is not part of the routine, although it appears to be just as effective as the preferred approach. But the teacher, a student teacher in this case, says, "You can try that way, but I'm going to do it this way."

On the next floor, an American government class, taught by a veteran teacher, is not much different. That teacher, too, leads students through routine exercises with little connection to the outside world. In this case, students are filling out a chart that indicates the political parties' position on major issues, such as taxes, a balanced budget, and education. For most of their information, the students consult the textbook. Only for issues for which the textbook lacks information, such as the balanced budget, do students seek out data from the newspaper articles that line the bulletin board. Even with the use of those articles, there is no indication that the class is taking place during an election year, when the positions of the political parties might have some relevance.

As every teacher and student in the school knows, these class-room activities and assignments lead to quizzes, papers, and tests that constitute the assessment of student learning at the school. The focus is on short-term learning of facts and techniques unique to that course, with very little attention to measuring students' deep understanding of key ideas; their cumulative progress on important skills in writing, math, or science; and their abilities to link ideas and strategies to the real world.

Perhaps the only exception to the rule of conventionality in curriculum and instruction is a science class taught by a young teacher who is involved in a national education reform effort. Ms. C., as all the students call her, has a relaxed, informal style. She tells jokes frequently, and plays sixties music while students work on laboratory experiments. But the work in her classroom is real science, and the students are deeply engaged in important content and scientific practices. For example, in one class, students investigate surface tension using simple materials: milk, food coloring, and liquid soap. The students are thinking like scientists, curious about what will happen if they vary the controls: "Let's try using a deeper container." "Let's try putting the food coloring in first and then adding the milk." They record all their observations, and are preparing to develop theories based on them.

Ms. C.'s class is evidence that the reform waves sweeping the nation managed to lap against GW's shores. But the fact that the class remains isolated from the prevailing practice proves that reform one teacher at a time is not enough to transform schools. The system in which the teacher works remains the same, and the system in GW's case militates against change. Curriculum design, textbook selection, and student assessment have little to do with each other in the reality of GW. Teachers advance up the pay scale at the same pace regardless of whether they are especially effective in helping students learn or even care about student success. The school and the district are awash in data about students, costs, programs, and personnel, but administrators do little to analyze the information to inform important decisions. There is little sense of accountability for student results, and no one seems able—even if anyone is willing—to improve the learning environment for students. Tradition is comfortable and satisfactory.

What's Wrong?

What's wrong with staying the same? Why should GW and other high schools want to change? After all, students graduate from the school and get jobs, most teachers feel they are doing the best they can, and parents and the community seem satisfied with their efforts. There is little clamoring for fundamental reform.

Beneath the surface calm, though, a number of troubling riptides threaten the prospects of the young people who attend the school. These features are hardly unique to GW; indeed, they are practically the rule in the 15,000 high schools in the United States.

Unclear Purposes Coupled With
Little Useful Information or Perspective

Like many high schools, and like shopping malls, for that matter, GW tries to be all things for all people. It is a social center, an athletics hub, a counseling clinic, a health provider, a driver training institution, a job preparation site, a luncheonette, and, oh yes, an academic institution. There is nothing that shows clearly that enabling students to reach high levels of achievement is the driving force of the school.

Moreover, if you ask people at the school how well they succeed in accomplishing their mission, they will be hard-pressed to answer. Plenty of information is available, but there is little evidence that teachers and administrators do much with the information once it is collected. For example, a counselor had to look through a couple of computer files and do some hand calculations just to determine how many students were enrolled in a particular mathematics class. There was no information on the performance levels of the students in the class. Everyone focuses on keeping school rather than seeking ways to improve results.

Low Expectations for Students

Many at the school talk about the relatively low expectations which teachers and parents hold for many students. In part, the teachers' expectations reflect the view many share that some students, by virtue of native ability, will succeed, whereas others, who lack innate intelligence, will not do well in school. The science teacher who grew up in the town expressed this attitude in this way: "We expect some will do very well and some won't do very well and some will do [average] . . . I do believe that there are average, below, and above average. The majority are average and if [a test] comes out that way I feel that [the test] must have been accurate."

Limited Parental Aspirations for Their Children

In addition to the teachers, many parents have limited aspirations for their children. As noted above, many students are aiming to become first-generation high school graduates. For their parents, a high school diploma is a signal achievement—as indeed it is. But they see no need for their children to pursue any education or training beyond the high school level. A high school diploma is good enough.

As a counselor in the school pointed out, some parents who hold such views declare their children financially independent after graduating from high school, thus making it difficult for them to afford postsecondary education. Largely as a result, many students who say they plan to go on for additional schooling change their minds during their senior year. As the counselor noted, financial reasons outweigh academic concerns in this decision.

Low Academic Standards and Grade Inflation

Perhaps because of the teachers' and parents' attitudes toward students, many teachers in the school set their academic sights rather low. GW's principal recognized this fact when he acknowledged that the number of As—about a third of all course grades were at this level—did not match the low test scores students received:

There is an underlying concern among the teachers to say, I don't expect what I did before. I'm not asking the same things I was asking 5 years ago or 10 years ago. Even the new teachers, the ones who have been there 2 or 3 years, feel it after a couple of years. It's like there's a push back when they say they want the kids to do the following things. At first the enthusiasm carries them and then up to a point it begins to wear on them. So that begins to lead to a feeling about what's worth fighting and what's not worth fighting. I think that may have some effect on the grades.

Teachers confirm the principal's hypothesis. Faculty members do not push their students too hard. One English teacher noted that her 12th-grade students balked when she asked them to write a term paper that analyzed a work of literature. "I never read a book before," the teacher said her students told her.

No Common Standards or Accountability

GW, indeed most high schools, allows teachers not to push because it lacks any kind of common standards. Teachers are free to close their classroom doors and make their own judgments about what constitutes good, or good enough, work. They are not held accountable for ensuring that students produce good work. They are not judged by how well students perform, only by how well they march through their own curriculum.

Moreover, the lack of common standards and accountability means that little support is available for students who are falling behind or are unprepared. Why should there be such support? Students can simply opt for a less demanding course sequence, or work less hard in their courses.

Weak Student Engagement

Students confess that they do not work very hard at George Washington High School. One student, a senior, admitted that he "coasted" through school. He noted that many students do, in part because the strong economy makes it likely that all students will get a job regardless of the education they receive. But he also pointed out that the school does not expect him and others to work hard. A student can fulfill the 2-year mathematics requirement and graduate by taking algebra and geometry, and going on to take trigonometry and calculus. Or a student can graduate after taking only basic math—essentially a review of elementary arithmetic—and consumer math, which teaches things like balancing a checkbook and determining payroll and wages. "Everything is so watered down because you've got people who don't care, they have to water their standards down so everybody can pass," the student said. "So people like me and other smart people, all they got to do is coast."

Anonymity

Although many students feel a close connection between themselves and the adults in the school because of the close ties between the faculty and the community, many others feel that teachers and administrators do not know them at all. They do not consider teachers as people they can turn to when they have a problem, either academic or personal, and thus receive little support from the school in their learning or their lives.

Student Alienation

Young people at GW are not disruptive, and in most classrooms, students appear diligent about their work, at least while they are in class. The one way many do act out, though, is by cutting class and cutting school, and the school considers attendance perhaps its most serious problem. In response, the school adopted a stringent policy that calls for strict monitoring of student attendance and disciplinary actions if students are absent excessively (defined as absent for a "significant percentage of a semester" and causing academic hardship). Many students bump up against this policy frequently. It is the one thing about the school students complain about consistently. And parents sometimes collude with their students to allow them to slip under the guidelines. If the school calls a parent to notify him or her that a student is absent, the parent will often offer an alibi for the student.

Students drift away from the school in other ways as well. The student who noted above that he coasted through school said he did so once he reached his course requirements; before that, he worked hard. Then he became more interested in his after-school job, and he spent his senior year taking only two courses (one was physical education) and spending the bulk of his time working. So it is with many students. Even extracurricular and cocurricular activities lose their appeal when students get older and want simply to pass through and get their ticket punched.

Ineffective Curriculum and Instruction

The teaching practices at GW are problematic not because they are traditional—tradition by itself is no sin, of course—but because they are based on an outmoded theory of teaching and learning. The heavy reliance on textbooks suggests that teachers accept the notion that if they march through the curriculum and cover as much material as possible, students will learn what they need to learn. The results show, however, that this has not worked.

Decades of research on student learning point to a different approach: Instruction should begin with clear expectations of what students should know and be able to do, and should provide students with opportunities to demonstrate their understanding in increasingly complex ways until they meet those expectations. Based on this research, schools at the forefront of improved learning are setting clear, high standards for student performance and making those standards—including examples of student work that meets the standards—prominent in classrooms. They then design courses of study that will enable students to reach the standards, and fill the courses with assignments that teach students the knowledge and skills they need and provide them with opportunities to demonstrate their learning. These courses add up to a coherent whole, unlike the unfocused, unconnected courses developed by teachers on their own.

A Breakdown in the Treaty
Between Teachers and Students

The calm that pervades the school and the lack of agitation for change does not imply that all is well. For one thing, the "treaty" that helps ensure quiet is fraying. As *The Shopping Mall High School* (Powell et al., 1985) describes, many schools, including GW, operate under a kind of treaty between students and the faculty. The adults agree not to push students very hard if the students agree not to be disruptive and get along. But at GW, although the teachers seem to be living up to their end of the bargain, the students are on the verge of breaking the deal. They are cutting school, registering their dissatisfaction and alienation not by active disruption but by refusing to participate. Just as low voter turnout is a worrisome sign for a democracy, low attendance signals serious problems in a school.

The school, meanwhile, is tugging at its end of the fragile rope. It is responding to the students' dissatisfaction not by increasing its demands but by imposing a punitive disciplinary policy. The school is not trying to break the treaty but to reinstate it. The result, though, may be the same: confrontation, but with little academic gain to show for it.

Lack of Incentives for Students

Right now, at least, employers in GW's town see little need to clamor for better-educated workers, unlike businesses in other communities. The unemployment rate in the city is low, and firms cannot find enough workers to fill jobs. All they want, they say, is people who will show up on time every day. Students hear that message loud and clear. They see that they can get high-paying jobs without taking difficult courses in school or getting good grades, and they know that employers never check to see what they know or are able to do. Many students get a taste of having spending money during school; they have part-time jobs that pay well, and because they live with their parents, their income is all discretionary. It feels good, and they can't wait to get out of school and to start earning more. They surely are not leading the charge to demand higher standards for student performance, and see no need to take tough courses or work hard at them. There is no incentive for them to do so.

But there is evidence that they are short-changing their future. The local community college offers training programs for high-paying careers, such as computer programming. But these programs are undersubscribed, in part because students lack the required skills to enter them and are reluctant to work as hard as they need to work to complete them. By taking advantage of the short-term easy money, students are missing opportunities for long-term gains that would be available with high skills and hard work.

An Uncertain Future

These problems are daunting. Yet they are not unique to GW. Far from it. They exist in one form or another in high schools throughout the United States, from inner cities to small towns like GW's to well-tended suburbs. As a result of these problems, millions of young people face an uncertain fate in a nation where so much depends on high levels of knowledge and skills.

In some respects, GW is better off than most schools. The school administration there has taken steps to institute a reform plan aimed at ensuring that students demonstrate performance to graduate. Attaining passing grades in 44 credits will no longer be enough to earn a diploma.

But the shift may prove to be a hard pill to swallow in the community. Virtually everyone at the school concedes that the performance levels of large numbers of students are far below what it will take to reach the standards. Will the community hold firm on the standards and allow large numbers of students not to graduate on time?

To make a performance-based system effective, the school— indeed, the school district, because the policy is in effect districtwide— needs to transform the system to ensure that students succeed. It needs to provide additional help to students who are falling behind. It needs to provide assistance to teachers to enable them to teach students in ways that will ensure that they can meet standards. It needs to reorganize the organization and management of the school so that the principal and the leadership team make decisions based on what students need to reach the standards. It needs to redirect resources so that the resources are concentrated on strategies that enable the school to achieve the desired results. It needs to engage parents and the public to support high standards for all students.

There is little evidence that the school has taken these steps. As a result, the school faces a dilemma. It can impose the performance requirements and watch for the fallout as large numbers of students are denied diplomas. Or it can water down the requirements and leave the system essentially as it is, with some students performing well and most doing just enough to get by. If it chooses the latter course, GW will remain the way high schools have existed for decades—just as Powell et al. (1985) describe and just as many counterparts remain to this day.

No school can afford the status quo. Fortunately, the keys to success are available. We know them from a substantial body of research and a substantial track record of experience over the past decade. This book outlines those keys. But first we must look more deeply into how high schools became the way they are and what has to happen in the next decade to fix them.

2

How Did We Get Here, and Where Should We Be Going?

Marc S. Tucker

The American High School in the 20th Century[1]

At the turn of the century, the high school was mainly for young people who were going to college. There were many fewer people in college then, proportionately, than now. Colleges were truly elite institutions, and so were the secondary schools that prepared young people to attend them. In those days, the standards and curriculum of the American secondary school were controlled by higher education. In the first two decades of the century, though, the nation's needs changed. The vast wave of immigration from poorly educated countries that had begun in the last century continued, and the burgeoning mass production revolution drove millions of barely literate people from farms to cities. The emerging jobs in the factories and assembly plants required people who were literate to a 7th- or 8th-grade level, a tall requirement for a country whose schools were taking in millions who were barely literate in any language. As the new labor unions gained strength, they voiced their interest in keeping young people out of the labor market, and they combined with business to create the idea of the modern trade and vocational school on the model of the British mechanics institute, a place in which young people could take courses preparing them for the skilled trades.

As the Second World War approached, all these separate elements found a home in the modern high school. The compulsory school age had been extended to 16 in most states. The high school had three separate tracks: one for the elite who would go on to get a baccalaureate degree and take leadership positions in the society, one for those who were training for the skilled trades, and one for everyone else, those who needed only the modest level of literacy required by the frontline jobs offered in the nation's factories and offices. African Americans had separate schools, including, in the big cities, elite high schools that prepared them for the few positions in management and the professions that were available. There were no dropouts, because it was expected that the only kids staying on through upper secondary school—the junior and senior year—were those in the academic track who were headed for college and those in some of the more demanding programs preparing young people for the skilled trades. Many of America's jobs were regularly filled by people who had never finished high school. For those who did finish, the high school diploma was a mark of distinction, and parents whose kids had received the diploma could hold their heads up high in the community.

All through this prewar period, there had been many competing views concerning the goals of secondary education. Among the most compelling, then and now, was the vision of John Dewey (1899) and others close to him in the Progressive education movement. Dewey's views were quite complex, and he was himself far from articulate in his expression of them. I can do no more than caricature those views in a sentence or two. But what is important for this discussion is Dewey's commitment to the idea that fully functioning adults require a high school curriculum that is not the arid elitist academic one inherited from the old prep schools, but rather a curriculum that, although intellectually demanding, also develops in students the capacity to function knowledgeably and responsibly in an increasingly complex society that demands much of them as citizens, workers, and family members. But Dewey's ideal was quickly corrupted, not least by those who regarded themselves as his strongest supporters, into a "life adjustment" movement that combined with a "child-centered" movement to produce a curriculum of little intellectual substance, a curriculum whose principal purpose seemed in the end to be to keep children in school by asking very little of them and providing a smorgasbord of offerings that offer something of interest for everyone.

The immense increase in the birthrate following the war put enormous pressure on the schools to accommodate the population boom. Among the most potent influences on the high schools in these years was the Carnegie-funded Study of the American High School, led by James Conant (1959, 1967). Perhaps Conant's most enduring— and hardly benign—legacy was his insistence that high schools had to be large enough to be able to offer a comprehensive curriculum that includes specialized courses in the sciences, mathematics, and so on. The small high schools that dotted the prewar American landscape could not possibly offer posts to the kinds of well-prepared teachers with the skills and knowledge necessary to teach these subjects well, but this argument paved the way for the monumental, anonymous institutions that characterize the current scene.

The postwar years also witnessed a vast expansion of higher education. Up to that time, one could rise to the top of the nation's business and social strata relatively easily without a college degree, but not so after. With these changes came a subtle but corrosive change in the public attitude toward schooling. Slowly, after the Second World War, the public came to adopt the view that only those with a college degree deserve real status in the social hierarchy. As the structure of the modern comprehensive high school evolved after the war, we completed its organization into a supermarket with something for everyone, but, with more determination than ever, we poured the available resources into those who were headed for college.

What was most corrosive, and what made it possible for us to organize what has become the most destructive tracking system in the world, was the American belief, aided and abetted by American psychology in the years just before and during the war, that academic achievement is a function of inherited ability, and only a small fraction of the population has the native intelligence required for serious academic work. In the years following the war, we perfected the tracking system based on the belief that only a few are capable of serious learning. The American high school became the keeper, the symbol, and the implementor of that system.

In the 1960s, the troubled conscience of the country, which had a decade earlier led us to abolish officially segregated schools, produced a new federal role in education, aid to the disadvantaged. The ideology of the time held that poor schooling was not the problem, but rather that the children brought problems to the school for which the schools had to compensate. The earlier the better, everyone thought, so the new aid for the disadvantaged went to the elementary schools and to preschool care and education, and not to America's high schools. With the abolition of officially sanctioned segregation, the nation's elite African American high schools were abolished and the African American educators who had staffed these schools were scattered to the winds in positions that made it difficult, if not impossible, to make the same contribution they had made before; inner-city high schools everywhere became the cauldron in which the racial fears and hatreds inherited over the decades took a terrible toll. So, although the country was beginning to make an effort to reverse the results of hundreds of years of slavery and discrimination, the effect on the high school experience of African Americans was ambiguous at best.

By the close of the 1970s, our high schools had become warehouses for young people in the general track everywhere. These students had neither hope nor expectation of going to a selective college, and knew that they could go to any community college or get a job with only a diploma. It was pointless to take a tough course or to study hard, because that would not change the outcome in any way. Everyone knew that the teachers would give their students a passing grade even if they did no real work as long as they did not cause much trouble, showed up regularly, and turned in their homework. The high school diploma, only a few decades ago a shining symbol of accomplishment, had now become merely a certificate of attendance. When graduation came, these kids would go and get the first no-skill dead-end job that came along. Sometime around the end of their twenties, they would start to take their first community college courses and get their first job on any kind of a career track. For these kids, maybe half the entire high school population, high school was simply time to socialize and tread water.

For the students—especially minority group youngsters—in inner-city high schools, the situation grew steadily worse, becoming a nightmare for many as the low-skilled jobs on which central city adults had so long depended went to other countries, and family economies became welfare dependency economies. The federal programs of the 1960s led in time to the labeling of millions of low-income minority kids as being in some way learning disabled. By the time they arrived at the door of the high school, there was no one—neither any adult nor they themselves—who believed that they were capable of serious academic achievement. Inner-city economic devastation was by then so complete that neither parents nor any other adult they knew was in a position to help them get a job of any kind when they left school. These youngsters thought it was hardly worth trying anyway, because employers would find the way they dressed and talked unacceptable when they applied for jobs in an increasingly service-oriented economy. Isolated, angry, and alienated from a world that had let them down in every conceivable way, they had only the gang to look to for support. High school for these kids was an expression of the society from which they were excluded. It was hardly surprising that high school teachers would come to school wondering whether one of their own students would shoot them that day.

But it was not just the general track that was in trouble. As the 20th century was drawing to a close, enrollment in vocational and trades programs was taking a nose dive all over the country. Whereas kids who aspired to be plumbers and electricians could take real pride in their chosen specialty years ago, this was no longer true. Increasingly, youngsters with ambition and resources decided on college and white-collar work; as they did so, the vocational and trades programs—like the general track—came to be viewed as a dumping ground for people with no future.

As the 1990s began, even the academic programs in the better suburban high schools seemed headed for trouble. The best of the best were as good as ever, but they accounted for a tiny proportion of the whole, and even here, teachers and principals often found themselves under enormous, irresistible pressure to give good grades whether their students deserved them or not. The students felt an unrelenting pressure not for real academic accomplishment but to get their tickets punched so they could get to the next stage in an increasingly competitive economy. Here, too, in all but the very best suburban schools, there was often no expectation that the students would do any work of real intellectual merit, and little opportunity for teachers to give their students the kind of personal support and criticism on which the development of high skill depends. Most youngsters in these schools, faced with the choice of working hard to get into a top-ranked college or doing just enough to get into a middle- or lower-ranked college, opted for the latter.

Despite teachers' best efforts, standards slid, and there was little they could do about it. There were and always would be young people of real ability who pushed themselves hard and achieved much, the kind of students all teachers would give anything to teach, but most of the college-bound youngsters were just going through the motions of completing a curriculum that rarely pressed them for deep understanding, that valued book learning far more highly than the capacity to do anything useful or even interesting with the knowledge they had gained, that failed to recognize the subtle interdependence between doing and understanding that Dewey (1899) had anticipated and modern cognitive science had revealed. These kids were just completing the rituals required of people who would eventually run our society, but getting far less out of the experience than they deserved or society required.

So, often for quite different reasons, most students from the inner city to the posh suburb are just going through the motions, and the modern high school has lost its moorings. Fundamental changes are needed in the basic structure of secondary education, changes that will give all students a reason to take tough courses and study hard, that will persuade students from low-income families and poor communities to believe in themselves and in their future, that will galvanize students from favored communities by setting challenges for them that they can and want to rise to and giving them a curriculum that matches those challenges. The talk in education circles is that the high school is the most resistant to change of all our educational institutions, and the least effective. The plan that follows would put the American high school in the front of the revolution.

The Challenge Now

We face a very different world now than America faced at the turn of the century. Whereas in 1900, three quarters of the workforce were expected—even required—to leave their heads at the factory gate, the American economy today requires workers at every level to think, reason, question, understand, and contribute—we need autonomous people who can lead and participate, who can challenge the existing goals and ways of doing things, and figure out what is worth doing and how to do it better. For the first time in this century, what employers most need is what school people have always said they want high school graduates to do and be. The transformation in the demands of citizenship have been no less striking—whether what is needed is an understanding of the dynamics of world population growth or an appreciation of the relationship between democratic liberalism and economic growth in the developed and developing worlds. Whether the issue is economic opportunity, democratic responsibility, or opportunities for personal growth and development, the demands being placed on our high school graduates are incommensurate with those faced only a few years ago.

The overwhelming challenge facing the American high school is to do a first-class job of the new basics—to make sure that all students really master the academic subjects in the core curriculum and are able to apply what they know to the kind of real-world, complex problems they will routinely encounter as adults. If that is to happen, the standards that students must meet will have to be defined, the students will have to be motivated to take the necessary courses and to work hard enough to meet the standards, and the schools will have to have the resources needed to get these motivated students to the standards.

A Certificate Standard for the New Basics

Imagine for a moment that across the United States a common standard exists for what American students should know and be able to do by the time they leave high school. Suppose that the standard is as high as the standards in countries that ask and expect the most of their high school students. Now suppose that it becomes the job of every high school in the United States to get its students to that standard, and the job of every student to reach it. Let's say that the standard is set at about what the students in the best-performing countries in the world can do in core subjects in the curriculum at about age 16. Some of our students would hit that target at 15, some at 16, and some at 18 or even 20. But all would be expected to hit it by the time they leave high school.

Bear in mind that we are not talking here about a standard expressed in the familiar form of a scaled score, but a standard that is in some sense absolute, like the standard set by lawyers' bar exams, pilots' license exams, or medical boards. It is a standard that one can keep shooting at until it is hit. The idea is not to use it to sort young people into bins of winners and losers, but to create a high standard for the new basics that all youngsters can and will hit, though some might do so earlier than others.

Say that the standards for the new basics demand that our students acquire both a deep understanding of the subjects studied and the capacity to apply what they have learned in the increasingly complex real-world settings they will face as adults. Say that the standards are set by a state or big city, which then issues a certificate—call it the Certificate of Initial Mastery (CIM)—to any student who meets the standards. Each jurisdiction would have to decide for itself what subjects it would include in the certificate standard and how it would assess its students against the certificate standards.

If it were up to me, the certificate standard would include reading, writing, speaking, mathematics, science, history, and applied learning (meaning nonacademic skills—such as problem solving, ability to use information technology and systems thinking—that are required in the modern workplace irrespective of the particular kinds of work to be done). This does not mean that other subjects—from foreign languages to the fine and applied arts—are not as valued or that the jurisdiction would not require students to take courses in those subjects to graduate, but it would mean that no student would get this certificate without reaching the specified standards in these subjects.

Many college admissions officers and employers would like to see a youngster's CIM before considering that person for admission to a college or hiring for a job with any career potential. As matters stand now, colleges and employers typically have no way of knowing whether a person applying for admission to college or for a job has mastered the basic knowledge and skill required for success in college or at work, unless that youngster has taken national exams set to known standards or the employer or college takes the time and goes to the expense necessary to administer its own exams. But if all the college or employer had to do was to ask for a certificate set to a known standard, most would do so in a minute.

Then students would know that to get a good job or go to college, they have to take tough courses and work hard in school. And that is just what they would do. This is not a guess. It is based on the evidence of what students do in countries that have clear standards that employers and colleges can use to make judgments about student competence.

The Certificate Program

Creation of the CIM will require a curriculum that provides a solid academic foundation for everyone. We envision a high school certificate program based on courses of study that make it clear, year by year, what the student has to study to do well on the certificate assessments. The courses of study would spell out what the designers of the assessments expect the student to have read in each course each year, what key assignments students must have had, and what topics they are expected to have covered. The courses of study would include examples of student work that met a comparable standard in prior years. Meeting the passing standard for the certificate would require getting a passing score in each subject and then accumulating additional points in one or more of the subjects. In turn, the score in each of the subjects would be based in part on end-of-course exams and in part on grades received on key pieces of work assigned through the year.

What I have just described is the way the CIM would work in high school. The same certificate, though, should be available to adults both young and old who are out of school and, possibly, in the workforce. For these people, exams set to the same standards should be available that would enable them to get the CIM by "testing out" of it. It should never be too late to get the certificate.

No system could be fairer. Every student would know just what is required for success, as would the teachers. Every student and teacher would know just what curriculum resources are necessary to do the required work. Every student who fails to get the points needed for the certificate on the first try would have repeated opportunities to try again, until the standard is reached. This is not a sorting idea; it is an idea for a system that produces very few failures.

This will challenge us to create a curriculum that provides a solid academic foundation enabling everyone to go on to a true college-level program, but alternatively to pursue, if they wish, a demanding program of professional and technical studies that may not require a 4-year college degree. It also will challenge us to abandon a system of credentialing of high school students based on seat time and courses taken in favor of one based on real accomplishment—on reaching a high, absolute standard of achievement.

By setting one standard for the new basics that everyone is expected to meet, the American high school will in one stroke abandon the insidious tracking system that has for so long denied opportunity to so many in favor of a system that guarantees opportunity for all.

If we can do all these things, then the American high school will be restored to the pride of place it once had in the American education system. The question is how to get there.

Refocusing the New American High School

The idea of a common, high standard, the same for all high school students, regardless of the path they then choose to take, is the fulcrum for redefining the American high school as an institution that focuses on one and only one task—bringing every student up to the highest academic standards possible.

The path that led the United States to the shopping mall high school has already been described. No comprehensive high school in America does a first-class job of bringing all its students up to either a high academic standard or a high standard of vocational skill. Some do one, some do the other, most do neither well. Our most admired high schools typically provide a fine college preparatory program, but provide a program for the non-college bound (if there are any such students at all) that is not the same source of community pride as the college prep program. Some communities have fine vocational and technical high schools, but they are typically competitive admissions schools that leave out the students in the bottom third or half of the distribution altogether, and they do not provide a college prep program at all.

There are two messages here. The first is that specialization pays off. First-class high schools get that way by focusing on doing one thing well. The alternative is doing many things badly. The second, hardly news, is that the bottom half of the distribution of students is served by neither the first-class academic high schools or the first-class vocational high schools.

Assume for the moment that our high schools adopt the certificate idea and commit to graduating all their students with at least the skills expected of 16-year-old students in countries where performance is highest. That is a much higher standard than is needed to get a high school diploma now almost everywhere, and it is therefore a higher standard than is needed to get into virtually all community colleges and many 4-year colleges. But it is not high enough to get into most selective colleges.

The first job of the new American high school should be to bring all its students up to the certificate standard. The second job should be to provide a first-class college prep program for students who have received their certificate and want to prepare themselves for competitive college entrance exams. These programs could be made up of Advanced Placement (AP) courses, the International Baccalaureate (IB) program, or other similar offerings.

That is all. And it is enough. It will be very hard for American high schools to bring all their students to the certificate standard and provide a first-class college prep program. To do that much is to ask more of our high schools than all but a few have been able to do up to now.

What, then, should be done for the millions of students who will prefer, after they get their certificate, to get a professional and technical education that may not require a baccalaureate degree at the entry level? When the certificate program is in place, everyone who wants to should be able to go on to a true college prep program, but alternatively to pursue, if they wish, a demanding program of professional and technical studies that may not require a 4-year college degree. Where are they to go if the comprehensive high school is abolished, as it should be?

Work and Schooling

Before that question is answered directly, it might be worthwhile to reflect a bit on the relationship between education and work for young people over the millennia. For most of human history, adolescence has been a time of initiation into the responsibilities and rewards of adulthood. For thousands of years, young people learned what they needed to know about work and acquired the values as well as skills they needed to do it by working with their parents and other competent adults. Education, training, character building, and work were all fused together into one.

This system, whatever its eventual limitations, had three enormous benefits. First, the work gave meaning to the education and training. It was obvious why one had to learn the skills that were being taught. Second, the constant interplay between work and learning provided a context in which learning and real understanding were the products of that interplay, not just the instruction by itself. The work provided the context in which understanding as well as meaning could grow. Third, growing responsibility gave meaning to the lives of young people as they took on the mantles of adults. By becoming useful, even indispensable, contributors to the larger community, the young people acquired value in the community's eyes and therefore their own. They were somebody they could be proud of.

Almost all these benefits of the ancient ways were lost when the modern secondary education system was built. For most of this century, American high school teachers, apart from those teaching explicitly vocational courses, have been deeply resistant to the idea that preparing young people for work was a major responsibility of the school. Given the mind-numbing quality of most jobs in the American frontline workplace, along with the desire of a great many employers for employees who will "leave their heads at the factory gate" and do as they are told, this attitude of teachers was quite understandable; they saw their duty as giving their charges a far wider window on life than their future employers thought they needed or wanted.

But all that is changing fast. Low-skill jobs are disappearing at increasing speed. The higher-skill jobs that are proliferating require the very qualities that good educators have always valued: broad and deep knowledge, a critical mind, the capacity for autonomous and thoughtful behavior, the ability to relate productively to others, the ability to think well, and the capacity to learn what one needs to learn when one needs to learn it.

It is also true that the cognitive scientists are teaching us something that John Dewey (1899) believed decades ago, that most knowledge is gained best in an environment in which we are using it to some real purpose. This interplay between work and learning produces better work and better learning. Our comfortable school folklore says that this is true only for the kids who are no good at academic work, the so-called hand-minded. But that is not what the cognitive scientists have learned. They know that it is true for most, if not all, of us.

For the kids who are now in the lower half of the distribution, especially those who are poor and from minority groups, a web of connections between school and workplace may spell the difference between success and failure, first in school and then later in life. For these kids to succeed in school, they must first believe that they have a chance of succeeding in life. Getting them involved early in high school with employers who show them how to succeed in the workplace, and giving them a chance to experience that success, may be the only way to engage these kids in serious academic work. One has only to see high school kids whom everyone has given up on trying to read a repair manual to fix a machine for which they are responsible to see how powerful this point is.

Connecting School to Work—For Motivation and Support for Academic Achievement

Picture for a moment a 14-year-old inner-city youngster engaged in a program that provides part-time employment that she will lose if she does not stay in school and make progress; mentors at the workplace whose job it is to help her be a success on the job; and tutors recruited from that same workplace who see their role as helping her succeed in school. Also picture an advocate whose only job is to get to know the mentors, tutors, parents, teachers, parole officers, and other adults in that youngster's life—but most especially the young person herself—and to be there for her, whatever it takes, to be that person who believes she can go the distance; expresses that faith; and helps her reach her goals.

Not all youngsters will need that kind of intensive support. But for many young people, especially those living in or near poverty and those for whom the academic work makes sense only in the context of the work they do, building links between education and work will be an indispensable element in getting to the certificate standard. The point has nothing to do with providing vocational training, steering young people toward particular careers, or providing them with particular vocational skills. It has to do with providing young people with the motivation and support they need to reach a high academic standard before they make any choices as to what career they want to pursue.

Connecting School to Careers—To Acquire Professional and Technical Skill

Now imagine that our high school student has completed all the elements of the required performance assessment with flying colors and gets her certificate. She's done well in advanced algebra, discrete math, and statistics. She can write an analysis of the politics, science, and economics of pollution control in her community that would commend itself to the mayor's top policy aide. And she won second place for her acting in a new play in the annual regional competition.

She has the option of staying in her high school in the college prep program to prepare herself for the SAT or American College Test (ACT) and the AP tests. But, like the majority of her high school classmates, she elects instead to choose a broad occupational arena, in this case precision manufacturing, and acquire the skills needed to get a good entry-level job in that arena, the start of a promising career in that field, one that could go all the way to chief executive officer of a big firm. She knows that, if she takes that route and gets a certificate in precision manufacturing, she will have only 2 years to go beyond that to get a baccalaureate degree in engineering. She is 16 years old.

The high school she goes to used to be a comprehensive high school, but is no longer. It is working hard to get its students to the new certificate standard as soon as possible. It offers a college prep program for those who want it, which is about a third of those who get the certificate.

The high school has a very close relationship with the local community college and the technical college. Both have articulation agreements with the state college system. Both have programs involving a mix of classwork and employer-based training leading to employer-developed occupational skill certificates that often come with associate degrees. They require all entrants into their professional and technical programs to have achieved the standard required for the Certificate of Initial Mastery. For adults who want to get an occupational certificate but who do not have a Certificate of Initial Mastery, they offer programs leading to that certificate.

In this case, the high school student who has just received her certificate learns that the technical college has a new program in precision manufacturing designed by college faculty together with a team of representatives from local manufacturing firms. The curriculum was framed to enable students to reach the national standards for precision manufacturing set by the national manufacturing partnership. Most students, she is told, should be able to get the precision manufacturing certificate and an associates degree from the technical college in 3 years. About half of that time will be spent in classes at the technical college and half at one or more of the firms in the local manufacturing education consortium. The program has also been designed to lead directly to the manufacturing degree program at the state college, but our student thinks that she will want to work full-time at least for a while when she gets her precision manufacturing certificate before going back to college for a baccalaureate degree.

What, exactly, is the new American high school as described in this scenario? The institution that carries that name has been redesigned and reconceived as an institution whose first and only job is academics—to make sure in the first instance that all the youngsters it takes in leave with the new certificate and the high level of academic skills that it attests to, and, in the second instance, to provide for those who want it, a first-class college prep program.

But the college prep program is not all there is to the upper secondary school. For many, perhaps most, students, upper secondary education now takes place in programs that combine classes taken at the local community college or technical college with employer-based training designed to complement the class work. These programs are all designed to articulate with 4-year college programs so that students who choose this path can go to 4-year colleges if they want to. All students who get their certificate from the high school can go to a 4-year college and most probably will, sooner or later.

The details of this description of the relationship between work and school are not important. But the broad features certainly are: First, its rhythm is keyed to standards, the certificate standard all students are supposed to meet, and then skill standards set by employers. Second, this is not a description of a work experience program but rather of an approach to education in which work and schooling are interwoven and the experience at work is explicitly conceived so as to advance the student's progress toward educational goals. Third, the experience for the student combines work, high school, and college in one seamless activity that recaptures everything that was lost in the early years of this century, when we severed work from formal schooling.

Why These Ideas About the
New American High School Are Important

The certificate idea is designed to strike at what we take to be the heart of the problem. For more than 70 years, the high school has both capped and served to legitimize the American tracking system, the very keeper of the idea that few kids have what it takes to do serious academic work. This proposal would stop that idea—the tracking idea—cold. It holds up the goal of the same high target for all youngsters, not different targets for different youngsters. All youngsters would have real choices after high school; the high school would no longer be handing out messages about who the losers are and who the winners are. It would no longer hand out a ticket punched for time in the seat, but would instead start handing out a ticket punched for accomplishment. Up to now, the message has been that society expects very little of most people—and that is what society gets. Imagine if we said we expect a lot of everyone, and we are going to get it.

Everything would change. The comfortable agreement that the student will get good grades for not causing too much trouble would end, because the student would know that good grades result only from good work. The student who is now in the general curriculum would be highly motivated, for the first time, to take tough courses and to study hard because that would be the only ticket to success later on. Teachers who always faced unmotivated students who were just "doing time" would for the first time face students eager to learn. Parents who stormed into the principal's office demanding that a failing grade be changed to a passing one would now become the teacher's ally, supporting both teacher and student as they struggle to succeed against a standard set from the outside that cannot be changed.

Teachers would see their job very differently. The oft-intoned message that all kids can learn would become the basis of official policy. The issue would no longer be the distribution of grades but how many kids at what age levels reach the high certificate standard set for all.

We would put behind us forever the notion that only some of us have to think and the rest can be content with doing, the distinction between the head-minded and the hand-minded that Dewey (1899) deplores and that became the excuse for creating a vacuous curriculum for the vast mass of our students. We would commit ourselves to an intellectually demanding curriculum for everyone. At the same time, we would embark on a mission this country has never attempted before, combining a curriculum for the head with one for the hand, doing as our ancestors did when they created contexts for the initiation of the young that called for them both to think and to do, all at once, intertwined. We would abolish vocational education as we know it and at the same time give it new life as an essential element in a new form of upper secondary education that is not an alternative to higher education but rather incorporates higher education. In doing so, we would restore the dignity of work that does not require a baccalaureate degree, while at the same time offering an opportunity for everyone to go as far up the educational ladder as they choose, at the pace that suits their circumstances.

We would redefine equity not as access to the curriculum but rather as success—whatever it takes—against an explicit, absolute curriculum standard that is as high as any in the world. This idea takes only a sentence to express, but it conveys an entirely different commitment to those who have had so little for so long.

Reform of the high school along these lines could be the driving force in a program that will transform the work of elementary and middle schools by changing forever the expectations for students entering high school; it will work an equally profound transformation of education, training, and work after high school by creating wholly different expectations for what kids should know and be able to do and how the institutions of our society should collaborate to help our young people satisfy those expectations.

Note

1. This brief and highly idiosyncratic account of the development of the modern high school cannot possibly do justice to this very complicated topic. Among the works in this arena worth consulting are Callahan (1962), Conant (1959, 1967), Cremin (1964), Hofstadter (1963), Powell et al. (1985), Marshall and Tucker (1992), Sizer (1985), and Tyack (1974).

Part II

*The New
American High School:
A Standards-Driven
Experience*

3

Standards and Assessment
The Foundation of
High Student Achievement[1]

Robert Rothman

THE IDEA OF setting high standards for student performance and developing assessments that measure performance against the standards is now commonplace among educators. This is no accident. School reform is aimed at significantly enhancing student learning, and standards and assessments are at the heart of that endeavor. Of course, standards and assessments are only the first step; the goal is to bring all students to the standards. But without this first step, all other steps will fall short, and student learning will not reach the ambitious heights envisioned by the Certificate of Initial Mastery (CIM).

This is because standards and assessments define learning and how we know whether students have learned what they need to learn. Standards define what we expect students to know and be able to do—the content we expect them to master, the skills we expect them to acquire, the intellectual qualities and habits of mind we expect them to develop. As Chapter 2, "How Did We Get Here, and Where Should We Be Going?" notes, the standards are for all young people—the skills and knowledge needed for effective citizenship are the same as those needed for a productive work life. In that way, standards help ensure equity by setting high expectations for every student.

Assessments linked to the standards, meanwhile, define the ways students can demonstrate that they possess the knowledge and skills the standards demand. They make the standards concrete. The results show the extent to which students, schools, and school districts are making progress toward the standards.

At their best, standards and assessments are more than just the necessary first step toward improved student learning. Properly done, they do more than define expectations for learning and gauge progress toward those expectations; they help students, parents, teachers, and members of the community enable students to learn at much higher levels. By setting clear, visible targets for performance, standards help students achieve at high levels by providing models of what good performance looks like. Likewise, stimulating and engaging assessments improve student learning, not just measure it, by providing students with opportunities to perform tasks that challenge them to use their knowledge and by providing teachers with examples of the kinds of performances students can produce in their classrooms day after day.

At the same time, a standards and assessment system makes it possible for classroom, school, and district efforts to improve student learning to move in the same direction—for the first time. Standards provide a common vocabulary that enables teachers and administrators at all levels to understand the expectations for student learning and what it takes to produce those levels of learning. Assessments provide a common measuring instrument that enables educators to understand how far they have come in achieving their goals and how far they have yet to go. By using these tools, teachers, principals, and district administrators can direct resources where they are needed.

What Are Standards?

The word *standards* has been bandied about so much in the education reform debate that many people remain confused about what the word actually means.

In part, the confusion stems from the different ways the word is used in ordinary language. One common use of the term is synonymous with criteria; standards are the way we measure the quantity of something. For example, the federal agency formerly known as the National Bureau of Standards (now the National Institute of Standards and Technology) determined how much gold constituted an ounce and how much wire made up a foot. These standards ensured that all machine tools that purported to be the same size were in fact identical.

But the origin of the term conveys a different notion. According to *Webster's* (1963), a standard is "a conspicuous object (as a banner) formerly carried at the top of the pole and used to mark a rallying point especially in battle or to serve as an emblem" (p. 853). Thus, in this sense, a standard is a point to which to aspire, not a gauge used for measurement.

This idea of standards—as a rallying point—is the notion that education reformers favor. They see standards as visible goals for performance to which all students aspire. The measurements determine how close or how far students are from reaching those targets.

In this respect, standards are new for most schools and school systems. Many schools have goals for students, but for the most part only a few students are expected to reach lofty goals. The rest of the students—the vast majority—are expected to lag behind and do as well as they can.

Moreover, these goals are seldom explicit; they are not standards in the sense that all students can see them and reach for them. Textbooks are brimming with content, but the concepts and skills students are expected to come away from a unit with are listed in the teacher's edition, not in the student books. Tests are deliberately kept secret, to preserve security, yet because of that, students do not know what they are expected to know and be able to do.

Some students, those who consistently do well in school, can thrive despite such secrecy. They have a sense, honed from repeatedly producing high-quality work, of what good work looks like and what they have to do to continue to produce it. Other students lack such an understanding. They get papers back from the teacher that indicate that they have fallen short of the mark, but they are not quite sure what the mark is. Nor are they sure what they have to do to reach the mark. For them, the standard might well be buried in the ground.

Even among those who accept the idea of standards for student performance as explicit goals for all students, there is some confusion about what a standard looks like. Thus, the many standards documents produced over the past few years—the national subject area standards, like the ones developed by the National Council of Teachers of Mathematics (NCTM, 1989), as well as state standards—vary widely in form and content.

This confusion stems in part from differences over what the standards documents are expected to accomplish. Are they for teachers, to provide guidance for developing lesson plans? Or are they for students as well as teachers, to help young people achieve at high levels?

Most of the standards developed over the past few years accomplish the first purpose but not the second. Most are content standards. *Content standards* outline the concepts and skills students should know and be able to do and the levels of schooling—elementary, middle, or high school—at which they should demonstrate understanding.

Content standards are valuable in helping schools and districts make judgments about curriculum. For example, the NCTM (1989) standards have been extremely influential in moving schools to place a greater emphasis on mathematical problem solving and mathematical communication. The math standards have also led schools to introduce concepts such as statistics and probability in earlier grades.

As important as content standards are, though, they are less useful in providing guidance to assessment developers, teachers, and most important, students to help them determine the appropriate quality of student work. For those types of judgments, performance standards are valuable. *Performance standards* indicate the level of performance students should demonstrate. They answer the question, how good is good enough?

The performance standards developed by New Standards (1997) answer this question not only by indicating the knowledge and skills students should demonstrate, but by citing examples of activities students can produce that demonstrate such abilities and—most important—including samples of student work that illustrate standard-setting performances. These samples are accompanied by commentaries that describe the circumstances of the performance (such as whether it was done in class or at home, or as part of a timed assessment) and annotate the work to show how it meets the standards (see Figure 3.1).

Performance standards complement the content standards and provide the guidance students need to produce work that meets standards and the guidance teachers need to design learning environments that regularly elicit such work. The performance standards,

English Language Arts Standards

1. Reading
2. Writing
3. Speaking, listening, and viewing
4. Conventions, grammar, and usage of the English language
5. Literature
6. Public documents
7. Functional documents

A piece of student work that demonstrates achievement of the standards was produced in response to a task in which students were asked to read and respond to a newspaper article, and to pay particular attention to the way the article was written and the implications underlying the arguments. In the response, the student wrote about an article on home schooling.

This piece met the standard for public documents, which states that a student "critiques public documents with an eye to strategies common in public discourse, including: effective use of argument; use of the power of anecdote; anticipation of counter-claims; appeal to audiences both friendly and hostile to the position presented; use of emotionally laden words and images; citing of appropriate references or authorities."

The work shows that the student responded responsibly to points with which the student agreed and one with which the student disagreed. The student also appealed to friendly and hostile audiences and concluded with an emotionally charged phrase—that a dance at a church function "doesn't hold a candle to the Senior Prom."

Mathematics Standards

1. Number and operation concepts
2. Geometry and measurement concepts
3. Function and algebra concepts
4. Statistics and probability concepts
5. Problem solving and mathematical reasoning
6. Mathematical skills and tools

Figure 3.1. Performance Standards

7. Mathematical communication
8. Putting mathematics to work

A piece of student work that demonstrates achievement of the standards was produced in response to a task that asked students to read a passage from a magazine article and to use mathematics to assess the article's claim that 40,000 words were uttered in a 200-mile train journey.

In the response, the student estimated the rate of speed of the train and the rate of speed of speech, and calculated the amount of time it would take to travel 200 miles and the amount of time to speak 40,000 words. The student concluded that the statement in the article was not reasonable, "unless he was intentionally speaking very fast, or the train broke down or stopped for an unusual amount of time at one of its stops."

This work demonstrates an understanding of geometry and measurement concepts, since the student uses quotient measures, such as speed, and could perform unit conversions. The work also demonstrates an understanding of function and algebra concepts, since the student found the time of travel and speaking rate by using formulas. The work also meets the standards for: problem solving and mathematical reasoning; formulation, since the student read the passage, focused on what was relevant and formulated and solved a particular problem; mathematical skills and tools, by estimating the values, in appropriate units, of quantities; and mathematical communication, by representing mathematical ideas effectively in writing.

Science Standards

1. Physical sciences concepts
2. Life sciences concepts
3. Earth and space sciences concepts
4. Scientific connections and applications
5. Scientific thinking
6. Scientific tools and technologies
7. Scientific communication
8. Scientific investigation

Figure 3.1. *(Continued)*

To illustrate a standard-setting performance in science, the standards documents include a paper written by a student asked to write a report on the benefits and risks in common medications. In the example, the student compared aspirin, acetaminophen, and ibuprofen by conducting an "interview" with each of the pain relievers and asking them to discuss their various properties.

This work demonstrates an understanding of life sciences concepts, specifically the behavior of organisms. The student shows an understanding of homeostatic mechanisms on bleeding by showing aspirin's effects on these mechanisms; an understanding of system control and maintenance by describing the effects of overdose on the nervous system; and an understanding that human systems are regulated by the production of chemicals.

The work also meets the standard for scientific connections and applications, specifically health, and most especially, for scientific communication. The student presents data and results through creative writing, argues from evidence, explains scientific concepts, and communicates in a form suited to the purpose and audience.

Figure 3.1. *(Continued)*

together with the content standards, form the essential building blocks of a standards-driven school and school system.[2]

Starting With Standards

How do standards improve student learning? It has become a cliché that standards alone do not lead to high levels of student performance. Yet it is also true that high student performance cannot come about without standards. They are a necessary condition. By themselves, standards contribute quite a bit to improving student learning.

The most significant role standards play in enhancing learning is in making clear—to students, teachers, parents, and the community—the goals for learning. With a clear set of standards for performance, all students have a clear, visible target to aim toward—a banner to rally around. They know what they are expected to know and be able to do, and they have a vivid image of what high-quality work looks like. They can then assess their own work and determine whether it meets expectations and, if it does not, what they need to do to ensure that it does. That provides an internal motivation for students to work hard, because they will want to turn in high-quality work.

Making expectations clear to teachers, parents, and members of the community helps students achieve as well. When all teachers know what all students are expected to know and be able to do, their conversations focus on student work in relation to the standards. Rather than talk about the problems they are having with Johnny, teachers can discuss what Johnny needs to do to bring himself up to the standards and what the staff collectively can do to help him. Similarly, parents provide more focused help for their children when they have a clear idea of what students should know and be able to do.

At the same time, standards that are integrated across grade levels and across levels of schooling provide a coherence and a sense of direction in schools. With an integrated set of standards, students know that what they are expected to learn in elementary school is the same as what middle schools expect them to arrive knowing and able to do. Teachers know that students coming into class having met standards have met their expectations, and they do not have to begin by going over what is old ground for many students. And parents know that the expectations for students in one school are the same as those in the other part of town.

Assessments as Learning Tools

Just as with standards, there is a lot of confusion in the current debates over education around testing and assessment. In large part, this confusion is inevitable, because few people actually know what tests measure. This widespread ignorance, moreover, is intentional; to prevent students from gaining an advantage by seeing test items in advance, test makers and school systems keep tests secret. As a result, people may advocate tests without knowing whether they help or hinder student learning. Depending on the type of assessment, a test can contribute to improved student learning, or it can do serious harm.

Many of the tests in place in schools now are harmful, for two related reasons: They are not tied to high standards for performance, and they place a premium on low-level knowledge and skills. As a result, classrooms that emphasize doing well on conventional tests—and these tend to be classrooms with large numbers of low-income and minority students—spend a large amount of time performing routine drills and little time enabling students to demonstrate their ability to use their knowledge and solve problems or to communicate their understanding. Students do not reach high standards in such classrooms.

Assessments linked to standards, by contrast, can improve, not simply measure, student performance by providing students with opportunities to demonstrate their understanding and by encouraging teachers to provide other, similar opportunities regularly as part of their classroom assignments. Rather than have students select from among a group of predetermined answers on a set of unrelated questions out of context, these standards-based performance assessments allow students to show that they can understand how to solve, say, a mathematics problem and can use mathematical language to do so. The results indicate not whether a student performs above the national average but whether the student has attained the standards.[3]

Assessments aligned with standards reinforce the learning advantages standards provide by offering students, teachers, and others greater opportunities to understand the expectations for student learning and the kind of work that meets those expectations. Assessments make the standards real by giving students opportunities to produce work that meets standards. At the same time, the criteria for scoring assessments spell out the expectations for students in greater detail. Students and teachers using those criteria know what constitutes a standards-level performance, one that exceeds the standards and one that falls short—and why.

It is for this reason that teachers say again and again that scoring assessments is the best professional development opportunity they have experienced. By seeing many examples of student work and judging them against standards, and by discussing these judgments with colleagues, teachers develop a clear understanding of high-quality student work, and, most important, of the kind of classroom environment they need to create to elicit such work from their students.

Likewise, students also benefit from understanding assessment criteria. They too develop a more vivid picture of high quality and the reasons why work meets standards for quality, exceeds standards, or comes up short. To illustrate the power for students of understanding assessment criteria, consider what happened in one middle school in

Kentucky. As part of a unit on the causes of the American Revolution, the teacher of a combined English and history class asked students to draw political cartoons that illustrated the British and colonial points of view about a particular event. The students at first were stymied, until the teacher showed them examples of similar work from the state assessment, along with the scores the work received. When the students saw top-scoring work and compared it with work that received lower scores, they were able to understand the characteristics of a high-quality piece and better able to produce one themselves.

Assessments that are "authentic"—that mirror real tasks, rather than situations cooked up solely for test purposes—also contribute to student learning by giving students challenging, engaging tasks that ask them to use their knowledge. An assessment that asks students to draw on content knowledge to solve mathematics problems or to demonstrate an understanding of historical trends is as much a learning tool as a classroom assignment that includes similar tasks. A portfolio system melds the two, classroom instruction and assessment, by basing the assessment on work produced over the course of the year.

Such assessments contribute to student engagement by enabling students to connect their work in school with the world outside of school. Schools that assess student performance through the use of projects and other long-range performance events have found that students care more deeply about their work, work harder, and perform better than they do in other types of assessments. In addition, the projects provide opportunities for students to work with adult mentors, who can show them how their knowledge and skills are used in the workplace and in their lives as adults.

A System of Standards

More and more educators are recognizing the educational value of standards and assessments, and are implementing them in some classrooms and schools. A CIM system, though, is just that—a system. It establishes standards, and assessments based on them, as the driving force across all classrooms and schools.

Perhaps the most significant advantage of such a standards-driven system is the alignment of classroom, school, and district goals for student learning. Currently, these goals are diffuse; they often conflict. The result is an inefficient use of resources, and an ineffective way of improving student learning.

Consider a typical example. A mathematics teacher sees that her students seem to do well in demonstrating conceptual knowledge, but less well in applying concepts to solve problems. The curriculum materials the district uses are stronger on conceptual understanding than problem solving, though, and she is eager to attend a workshop that will help her learn how to teach problem solving to her class. But she can get little help from the district, because the district does not see what she sees. The district test scores, based on a traditional test that includes many questions on conceptual knowledge and few on problem solving, are fairly high. The district has decided to focus its resources on English language arts, where test scores are lower.

In a standards-based system, there would be no conflict. The goals of the teacher and the district would coincide, and the measuring instrument would as well. The teacher and the district would be able to direct resources where they are needed—to help students reach the standards. And the students would know they are successful, when test scores rise.

A Standards-Based Assessment

What does an assessment based on standards look like? In some ways, it is difficult to answer this question. To state the obvious, it depends on the standards!

In that respect, standards-referenced assessment represents a sharp contrast to the type of assessment used in most classrooms today. Today, assessments are designed to compare students' performance to that of other students or that of a "norm group," who may have taken the test years before. The questions are general, not tied to any one curriculum or set of standards, and students—as well as parents and teachers—are told whether they score higher or lower than other students, not whether they demonstrate that they know and can do what they are expected to.

Standards-referenced examinations, on the other hand, set an absolute level of performance and report whether a student has met that level, rather than reporting where a student falls on a bell-shaped curve. Standards-referenced examinations begin with a very clear definition of the learning standards to be met—including multiple examples of student work that meets the standards. The standards are made available to test users—including teachers, students, and parents. Then the exam is systematically constructed to assess the extent to which individual students meet those standards reliably and validly.

To see an example of a standards-based assessment, consider the task depicted in Figure 3.2. The 45-minute task is designed to assess reading as well as writing.

End-of-Course Examinations

A key feature of standards-referenced examinations is that they are designed to be studied for. The standards are public, so students, parents, and teachers have a clear idea of what students are expected to know and be able to do, and can prepare students to do well on the exams. Although many educators shun "teaching to the test," considering it a form of cheating, students should see their classwork pay off in exam grades. They should know that if they read what they are assigned, do their homework, study regularly, participate in class, and so on, they will earn higher scores.

This is true for two reasons. First, students, teachers, parents, and the public should trust the assessment system. This trust is absent in the current system. Students consider the scores a reflection on themselves, rather than on their work, and many teachers—the ones who abhor teaching to the test—feel the same way. As a result, people consider the scores illegitimate, and thus are reluctant to hold themselves accountable for them.

With an assessment system they can trust, however, students, parents, and teachers know that the scores reflect the quality of the students' work and the opportunities and support teachers and parents provided. They know that a low score signals a gap in learning, and they will act to address it, rather than dismiss it.

The second reason students' class work should pay off in higher exam scores is to provide an incentive for students to work hard in school. As the first chapter of this book shows, high school students do not exert themselves much in school. They do what they need to do to get by, and they do not need to do very much. Why should they work hard? They are not asked to do much, and what they do in class does not matter beyond that assignment or that chapter in the textbook. If, on the other hand, students know that by working harder they will earn higher scores, and higher scores matter to them, they

---

English Language Arts Task

Reading Passage
  "Grant and Lee," by Bruce Catton

Reading Questions

1. According to Bruce Catton's article, Robert E. Lee and Ulysses S. Grant represented "two conflicting currents" in American life. Using Catton's descriptions of Grant and Lee, how do you think they might describe each other? Write a description for each one as viewed by the other.

   • A description of Robert E. Lee as viewed by Grant
   • A description of Ulysses S. Grant as viewed by Lee

2. According to the article, Lee believed there should be a "leisure class" which would be the source of "leadership" for the country: "a class of men with a strong sense of obligation to the community; men who lived not to gain advantage for themselves, but to meet the solemn obligations which had been laid on them by the very fact that they were privileged."

   How does Lee's belief contrast with Grant's view of American society and the place of the individual in it? Refer to details from the article to support your answer.

3. In this article, Bruce Catton draws a sharp contrast between Grant and Lee as representatives of "two diametrically opposed elements in American life." In drawing this contrast, does Catton reveal his preference for "one side" or the other? Or do you think he is fair in presenting the strengths and weaknesses of both? Explain.

Essay

   Catton calls Grant "the modern man emerging." Would you agree that Grant is more representative of "the modern American" than Lee? Explain, drawing on both Catton's text and evidence from your own knowledge or experience of modern life. Remember that your response to this question will help your readers see how well you write and how well you are able to think about your reading.

Figure 3.2. New Standards Reference Examination

will put a lot more effort than they currently do into high school. The students in the focus groups conducted by Public Agenda, in its 1997 report on high school students' attitudes toward school, said as much (Johnson & Farkas, 1997).

There is one place where high school students do work hard: in Advanced Placement (AP) courses. There, the work students do each day in class helps them learn what they need to know to do well on the AP examinations. Students know that, by doing well on the exams, they can earn college credit. That is why they work hard in class.

Standards-referenced examinations are like AP exams. They are end-of-course exams in which the exam measures performance on a detailed program of study, which is derived directly from the standards. Students who take the courses and study for the exams should perform well.

End-of-course examinations are similar to what is familiarly known as a final exam; that is, an exam where teachers and students are clear about what should be taught, what should be studied, and what should count as fair game in the end-of-course assessment. Unlike traditional final exams, though, the standards-based end-of-course examinations do not vary from class to class or from teacher to teacher. Instead, the district administers a common examination across a given grade level in a standardized manner. Scoring criteria, too, do not vary from teacher to teacher, because each end-of-course examination is scored using a common set of scoring criteria, based on the standards. Using this approach, the district can determine how well each cohort of test takers meets the standards.

Portfolios

As important as end-of-course standards-referenced examinations are, they are not the only method of assessment in a standards-based system. A timed assessment cannot measure student performance on all the standards without taking many days to administer. Some standards simply cannot be measured through on-demand assessments—for example, the ability to complete a complex laboratory experiment.

To complement the examinations, standards-based systems use portfolios. For teachers, portfolios offer two major advantages. First, they help teachers organize the curriculum. A teacher knows that the goal is to enable students to produce work that can be entered in the portfolio. Thus, he or she creates a sequence of assignments, based on the standards, that will enable students to produce such work.

Second, the portfolio helps bring the standards into the classroom every day. Portfolios provide a concrete way of ensuring that students see the work they are doing in class against standards, and helps them develop a clearer sense of what is "good enough." With that sense, students are better able to assess their own work, and thus better able to understand what they have to do to improve the quality of their work. They produce better work, and learn more, as a result.

To be effective, though, a portfolio cannot simply be a random collection of work. The link to the standards—both content and performance standards—is critical. For example, the English language arts portfolio should show work from each of the genres: reports, responses to literature, narrative accounts, narrative procedures, persuasive essays, and reflective essays. The quality of work should match the quality of the exemplars represented in the performance standards.

The High School Assessments

The assessment system in a standards-based high school begins before the ninth grade. As noted above, the standards-based system is designed to provide coherence across all levels of schooling and all schools so that the expectations for students are the same no matter where students happen to attend school. Similarly, the assessment system is aimed at determining whether students meet the standards and directing resources to help them if they fall behind so that they can remain on track.

For that reason, a key element in the assessment system is the 8th-grade gateway assessment. It is called a "gateway" because passing it opens doors for students into high school. It is designed to end the system of social promotion that has allowed thousands of students to enter high school ill-prepared for the work they are expected to complete. At the same time, it is not simply an unscalable barrier that locks lower-performing students into an endless cycle of repeating classes. Rather, it provides information to help students, parents, and teachers understand what they need to do to help young people keep up and learn what they need to be ready for high-school-level work.

The assessment therefore is linked closely to the high school end-of-course examinations. The syllabus on which it is based is developed in conjunction with the high school courses of study so that students who do well in 8th grade are prepared for the 9th-grade work. In that way, students who do well on the gateway assessment stand a good chance of succeeding in high school, unlike in the current system, when many are forced to sink or swim because of the variability of 8th-grade coursework. Teachers in the high school can develop a rigorous and engaging program, knowing that students are not handicapped by poor preparation.

The Certificate of Initial Mastery

The CIM is the culminating element of a coherent and integrated system of assessments based on standards. The CIM certifies that students have achieved high standards in core subjects; it is a certificate of accomplishment, not attendance. The CIM offers a real incentive, one lacking now in schools, for students to take challenging courses and to perform well in them.

To be a fair assessment of a student's achievement and serve as a basis for rewards, the CIM should consist of multiple measures of student performance. A single test, particularly one administered on a single day, is an inadequate gauge of a student's knowledge and skills. A single test measures only a fraction of the standards all students are expected to demonstrate. Many factors could contribute to a student's performance on one day.

To measure the full range of standards, and to provide students with opportunities to demonstrate to the fullest extent their knowledge and skills, the CIM should consist of three parts, all of which are linked explicitly to the standards: end-of-course examinations for grade 10; course assignments; and a capstone project.

End-of-Course Examinations

The end-of-course examinations represent a key component of the CIM because they measure student knowledge and skills on a clear program of study. They thus enable students who work hard on a rigorous program to do well.

But although the 10th-grade end-of-course examinations are the ones that "count" for the CIM, they are not the only exams students will take, nor are they the only ones that matter. Students do not learn all they need to know for a CIM in the tenth grade; far from it. The knowledge and skills they demonstrate in those exams are the culmination of years of learning.

Thus, the programs of study for the tenth grade are part of a sequence of programs of study that begins as early as the seventh grade. At the end of the earlier grades, students take diagnostic end-of-course examinations, which provide them and their teachers with an early warning signal of potential problems that might harm the ability to earn a CIM. With that information, students can enroll in summer or after-school programs to remain on course to earn the certificate.

Course Assignments

An on-demand assessment cannot measure student performance on all the standards. For example, it is unlikely that an on-demand assessment will allow students enough time to complete competent papers in all the genres called for in the *New Standards Performance Standards* (1997).

During the course of a year, though, students can write in all genres, and they can do so by revising their work and producing polished, high-quality papers. Including course assignments in the CIM enables students to demonstrate the range of their knowledge and skills as well as competency in extended work that is difficult to tap in a short, timed assessment.

In addition, including the course assignments on the CIM also ensures that the standards become a part of the everyday classroom experience. This will enable students to understand more deeply the expectations for their work, and thus be able to assess their own work and improve it. It will also enable teachers to understand what they need to do to elicit high-quality work from their students.

Capstone Projects

Capstone projects enable students to put what they have learned to work. Cognitive researchers say that students learn best when they apply their knowledge to real problems; employers say they want to hire young people who can use their knowledge. Capstone projects provide the opportunity for students to demonstrate that ability.

Capstone projects also enable students to demonstrate skills that cut across subject areas; abilities New Standards (1997) identifies as "applied learning" standards. These include problem solving, communication tools and techniques, information tools and techniques, learning and self-management tools and techniques, and tools and techniques for working with others. Like the standards assessed in the course assignments, these standards cannot be measured well in an on-demand assessment.

The purpose of the capstone project is to demonstrate the capacity to engage in an extended, in-depth line of work that is authentic to the field chosen. This means engaging with practitioners in the field, not only with teachers. A particular challenge will be to avoid routinized forms of school projects that do not engage students in the kind of work competent adults do.

Project work should be guided by a committee encompassing at least a teacher and a practitioner in the field the student is working in. The project should take about a semester to complete and involve substantial outside-of-school work. Most capstone projects should be designed by students, with the help of their committees, to reflect their particular interests and learning opportunities.

Students choose from among a menu of projects, much as Boy Scouts and Girl Scouts select merit badge activities from the handbooks. Like scouts, students earn credit toward the capstone cumulatively, from the beginning of high school, rather than on one major project at the time the student earns a certificate. The menu might include producing an oral history, making a map, staging a production, profiling a job, putting on an exhibition, and coaching a team.

The capstone assessment consists of an interview with a school-community panel. In the interview, the student is expected to use evidence from the project to demonstrate a key result drawn from each area of the standards and at least one area that shows improvement over the course of the project. The interview is designed to enable the student to synthesize knowledge and experience, using evidence from the projects to illustrate points, rather than to relate project narratives.

Earning a CIM

By taking the end-of-course examinations, submitting a portfolio of course assignments, and completing capstone projects, a student can qualify to earn a CIM. But because the key principle of the CIM is that it represents real accomplishment, the student cannot simply fulfill the requirements. Students need to demonstrate that they have met the standards. The scoring system shows whether students have done so.

One possible scoring system for the CIM is a point system. A student's scores on the exams, the course assignments, and the capstone project are compiled into a score for each subject; say, 1 to 5. A student's total score is the sum of the points in each subject. A student earns a CIM when his or her score exceeds a certain threshold; however, the score goes on the certificate to show higher education administrators and employers how the student performed in school.

The point system represents a way to ensure that all students demonstrate a common core of knowledge and skills, while at the same time allowing students to pursue areas in which they have particular interests and talents. The core is a key idea. A student cannot earn part of a CIM—say, in English, but not in mathematics, because he or she does not like mathematics. The CIM is a whole that represents standards common for all students. A student can earn a CIM in stages, however, and can earn "merit badges" that show real accomplishment in particular subjects and that a student is on the path toward a certificate.

At the same time, a student can excel in any area. Earning a CIM takes solid accomplishment, not superstar achievement, in all subjects. But the CIM allows a student, like the English specialist, to show talents in that area. In doing so, it gives students a chance to earn recognition toward the CIM as a whole for especially good work in some areas. It allows superior work in one subject to compensate for somewhat weaker performance in another—but it does not allow substandard work in any subject.

Although the point system represents one way of scoring a certificate system, schools and districts choose their own system, based on local needs but adhering to the CIM principles.

Incentives for Students

Why would a student go to the trouble? Earning a CIM is difficult, and students do not work hard in school.

We believe students will go to the trouble. First, simply putting a CIM in place will signal to students that the school expects more out of them than schools currently do, and students will rise to the challenge. That is what the students in the Public Agenda focus groups said, and there is ample evidence from experience to suspect that it is true (Johnson & Farkas, 1997). All the programs that produce high levels of achievement from students start with the premise that they expect all students to succeed; students hear that message, they know people believe in them and care that they succeed, and they do what is expected—and more. Raising expectations, by itself, would do a great deal to raise performance in high schools.

The CIM offers the possibility to add an additional incentive for students. If a student's post-CIM career depends on performance, the student will want to ensure that he or she works as hard as possible and performs as well as possible to open options for the future. This kind of external motivation is what makes the AP program so successful: Students work hard to earn college credit.

The redesigned high school described in this book offers opportunities for students that give them incentives to work hard for a CIM. The CIM serves as a kind of ticket for the pathways students can choose once they have demonstrated their abilities and earned a CIM. Yet, it is important to note, this is not because the CIM functions as a gatekeeper, but because the certificate demonstrates that a student has the knowledge and skills needed to succeed in the future.

For example, for a student intending to go on to college or university and who is enrolling in AP courses or the International Baccalaureate (IB), the CIM would assure teachers that the student has the knowledge and skills needed to do well in those programs. For a student planning to go into the workforce after school, the CIM would demonstrate that the student is able to succeed in the combined technical-academic coursework needed to earn a skill certificate.

Post-CIM Assessments

Both of these avenues for students—higher education and technical studies—culminate in assessments that also provide incentives for students to work hard and achieve much. The AP examinations, the culminating assessments in the academic pathway, are well-known. Like the end-of-course exams students take in the years leading up to and including the CIM, the AP exams are based on an explicit and carefully described course of study that makes clear the expectations for student learning during the year. If students complete their assignments and study hard, they will do well on the examinations. By doing well on the examinations, they can earn credit in most colleges and universities—before setting foot on campus.

Similarly, the IB includes end-of-course exams based on a rigorous course of study that is explicit and well-known. Students also complete independent study, analogous to the capstone project required for the CIM, to earn an IB. Like the AP courses, the IB is recognized by colleges and universities as equivalent to first- or second-year college courses, and most award credit to incoming students who hold IBs.

For those pursuing the technical route, the culminating assessment is based on skill standards such as those being developed by the National Skill Standards Board. These standards are designed to prepare students for a broad range of occupations in multiple industries that require similar skills. The assessments demand a deep understanding of the work performed in these occupations, and students are judged by both teachers and industry representatives.

These assessments also require academic knowledge and skills. The technical preparation pathway is not a track for those not bound for college or university; it is another way a student can go to a university. The academic requirements are rigorous enough to ensure that colleges and universities will accept students with these certificates.

Three Challenges

Implementing a standards-based assessment system is not easy. The United States has relied on norm-referenced testing, and has accepted the beliefs about the variability of student achievement it implies, for decades. Putting in place a new technology, with a new set of beliefs about the possibility of all students achieving at high levels, will be difficult. Putting in place an effective system poses an even greater challenge.

One major challenge in implementing standards and assessments is ensuring that people throughout the system, particularly teachers and students, have a deep understanding of the standards and the expectations they imply for students' knowledge and skills. Students will meet standards only if they and their teachers are able to use the standards day after day in the classroom to develop their abilities and improve their work until it reaches standards-level quality. Without a deep understanding of the standards, this will not happen.

One way to help ensure that this happens is through the use of student work. By providing, along with the standards, samples of exemplary student work, jurisdictions can make the standards concrete and bring into focus what it means to meet standards. Moreover, the examples reassure teachers and students that standards-level work is possible and that students have accomplished it.

Making these examples effective for teachers takes professional development. Teachers need opportunities for meaningful professional discussions around the work and its implications for their classrooms.

Some districts accomplish this task by holding conferences around their assessments, using tasks from previous versions of the assessments and student responses to these tasks as examples of standards-level work. Some hold discussions on cable television or through teacher newsletters. The Internet is a promising venue for discussions around standards and student work. By putting the standards on-line and debating them with teachers and students, schools can help everyone develop a deeper understanding of the kind of knowledge and skills students are expected to demonstrate, and thus make a start toward producing it.

A second challenge in implementing standards-and-assessment systems is ensuring confidence in the assessments. Educators generally agree that traditional tests provide an inadequate measure of student abilities, and that performance-based assessments and portfolios enhance the quality of information available about students' knowledge and skills. Yet many educators and public officials, as well as members of the public, remain skeptical about the accuracy of the results of the new assessments. Unless schools can erase those doubts, their ability to implement new systems is in jeopardy.

In many respects, these public doubts about new assessments are healthy. Traditional tests have been in use for decades, and have proven to be technically sound. Performance assessments, at least as external measures of student performance—those used by districts and states for accountability purposes—are relatively new. People are rightly concerned about whether a new instrument is "safe and effective," just as they would be with a new medical procedure. The concerns are particularly acute because the new measures appear more subjective, and reliant on teachers' judgment, than machine-scored standardized tests.

Although test quality is usually an arcane subject, parents and policymakers have shown an unusual interest in the technical quality of performance assessments, and in some cases their concerns have helped curtail a shift to new measures of student performance. In California, for example, an expert panel's report criticizing the California Learning Assessment System was a major reason behind the decision by Governor Pete Wilson to kill the program.

Although significant issues still remain, the good news for those shifting to new assessment systems is that districts and states trying out new methods are finding ways to improve the quality of the measures. Their success points to ways to build confidence in the assessments as they are implemented.

One sign of hope is that researchers are finding that new assessments can be scored much more reliably than before. Reliability has been a major concern with the new assessments, because a low level of reliability—agreement among raters on the score for a piece of student work—threatens confidence in a student's score. Researchers are finding that with a clear understanding of scoring criteria—supplemented by vivid examples of student work that meets the criteria—teachers can agree on the ratings to assign a piece of student work. Getting such an agreement, though, demands considerable professional development to develop the teachers' understanding of the standards.

Another sign of hope is that some jurisdictions, notably Kentucky, have modified their assessment systems to improve the technical quality without sacrificing their educational value. Kentucky's original assessment system was completely performance based, and included portfolios in mathematics and writing. But expert panels questioned the exclusive use of such methods to award cash rewards for high performance and to issue sanctions against schools for declining performance. In response, the state added multiple-choice items to the assessment mix and uses only the writing portfolios—which have a longer track record as assessments—as part of the accountability system. The result is a balanced system that includes a variety of measures of student performance. This is an appropriate response; there is no one right way to measure performance, as long as the assessments measure student performance against the standards.

The third major challenge is related to the second: securing public support and endorsement for standards-based improvement in education. In addition to questioning the use of new assessments, parents and members of the public are raising doubts about standards and using standards to hold students and schools accountable for performance.

In some cases, these questions stem from organized groups, who have attacked standards as attempts to institute *outcomes-based education*, a much-abused term that is now almost an epithet among some critics. To these groups, defining the knowledge and skills students should demonstrate represents an attempt to impose values on young people, which they consider an inappropriate role for schools.

At the same time, many parents and members of the public question whether standards represent an attempt by educators to evade responsibility over their primary concern: teaching "the basics." Because of the emphasis many educators place on developing students' abilities to reason and solve problems, some parents fear that the three Rs, which they consider paramount, might get lost in the shuffle.

Not many districts or states have responded effectively to such concerns. Some may have inadvertently fueled such concerns by adopting vague standards that sound less than rigorous or test questions that appear to be invasions of privacy. Those that have responded effectively, though, have won enthusiastic support from the public. They have succeeded by using the most powerful tool the new systems offer: student work. They show that the kind of work they expect students to perform in the new standards-and-assessment systems is the kind of work parents want to see their children produce. They show that children learn the basics while they perform complex mathematics tasks and write several-page essays. And they show that students are learning academic knowledge and skills, not being indoctrinated in values and attitudes.

Notes

1. Portions of this chapter are excerpted from Rothman (1997).
2. A number of organizations have produced reports that spell out the characteristics of high-quality standards; in a sense, these represent standards for standards. These include the American Fed-

eration of Teachers (1997), the Business Task Force on Student Standards (1995), the National Education Goals Panel, Technical Planning Group (1993), and New Standards (1997).

3. For more information about performance assessment, see Rothman (1995) and Wiggins (1993).

4

Rethinking Curriculum and Instruction in the New American High School

David D. Marsh
Philip Daro

TWO SALIENT FEATURES of this volume's overall design for the new American high school have far reaching implications for curriculum and instruction: the changes proposed in the structure of the high school and the key role that standards are meant to play in its design and ethos.

Curriculum for the Lower Division

There are several important implications of the structural design of the new American high school. At bottom, what has been proposed is a sharp and newly important distinction between the lower division in high school and the upper division. The lower division program has only one object—to prepare the student to meet the standard for the CIM or its equivalent. The student should not progress to the upper division program without the CIM, nor should the student get the high school diploma without the CIM or its equivalent. Once the student has the CIM, he or she can proceed to the upper division, choosing between a demanding college prep program designed to prepare the student for competitive college entrance examinations, or the professional and technical program, designed to prepare the student to meet demanding standards set by employer groups for the clusters of occupations. Students entering the second program participate in a program consisting of some high school classes, some community college (or technical college) classes, and one or more internships with employers, often during the summer months. These students will receive, in addition to the high school diploma, college credit, an industry skill certificate and, in some cases, a two-year college degree.

Which raises three questions: What should the curriculum be in the lower division for students pursuing the CIM? What should the curriculum be for students in the college prep program? And what should the curriculum be for the Professional and Technical Program?

A Standard Core Curriculum

Few would argue with the proposition that the lower division curriculum should include mathematics (including algebra, statistics, probability, geometry, and trigonometry), English language arts (including writing in a number of genres, as well as courses in literature), physics, chemistry, biology and history. To that list we would add art, music, geography, and health/physical fitness. We would have explicit external performance standards for each subject (including physical fitness), with matching performance assessments in each case, wherever possible.

What this amounts to is a standard core curriculum that is the same for everyone, with common standards that all students must meet to get their diploma, and to proceed to the upper division program. We would add to this list only a handful of electives, including, perhaps, economics, a foreign language and technology. The point of having a standard core curriculum is to focus the energy and attention of both teachers and students on what matters most, to the exclusion of everything else. It represents the opposite of the shopping mall high school and an essential step in building an effective antidote to the "mile wide and inch deep" curriculum identified by the TIMSS researchers and a leading cause of America's appalling performance on that international comparison of educational achievement.[1]

Concentrating on a few subjects, each of which has its own associated standards, makes it possible for the faculty to work together to build systematically the most effective courses for each subject and to work as a whole group, subject by subject, to devise the most effective instructional techniques to address the problems of specific students or groups of students. Because the courses are taught in common across the whole faculty, faculty members can analyze their practice together and learn from one another about how to address the most serious problems they face in their classrooms.[2]

Students who are not progressing well in the lower division program would concentrate exclusively on the core program. Those who were progressing nicely could take a few electives. Because the CIM—and access to the upper division program—would be based only on the core, the students who were taking more class time to master the core would not get as broad a program as the others, but they would be held to just as high a standard for the core as the other students.

It goes without saying that the English language arts curriculum would include literature and a heavy emphasis on writing. What may need some emphasis, however, is our view that the writing curriculum should be constructed so that the students master not one but rather a number of writing genres in which they will be expected to write as part of the work that they do, as well as the writing they do for enjoyment. The humble memorandum has its place alongside the poem and the short story, as does the document analyzing the failure of a machine and those documents written to provide instructions to others.

Perhaps the most surprising, and for many schools, most important challenge to be faced in English language arts is the poor reading comprehension of many students. Students who cannot comprehend the words on the page in class after class become angry, defeated, and usually alienated, and they often drop out of school. Typically, these students have a very limited English vocabulary, which is both a cause and an effect of their reading problem. In any case, though we have many high school English teachers, we have very few high school reading teachers. Because no high school curriculum set to high standards for all students can succeed if the students do not read fluently, this issue of reading may be the highest priority curriculum issue in many American high schools.

History—often called the "queen of the liberal arts"—has many uses, but not the least of them is the development in the student of an understanding and appreciation of the origins and structure of our form of democracy, the moral choices that have come before us as a people and the way they have been decided, and a context for deciding the issues that have yet to be decided.

In mathematics and science, we would argue that the central issue is providing a balance among basic skills and knowledge in the discipline, deep conceptual understanding, and the ability to apply what one has learned to real-world, complex problems.

A Balanced Curriculum

We have little patience with those who say that because there is so much new knowledge produced all the time, it is pointless to ask students to learn the facts—all that is needed is to provide the skills that they will need to learn what they need to know when they need to know it. Learning is like a coat rack and the coats. Each discipline is associated with a structure of knowledge in that field, a bit like the coat rack. Each new coat fits on the rack, just as each new piece of knowledge makes sense to us only to the extent that it fits in with what we already know and the other facts we already have. In fact, that is literally what it means to "understand" something. No structure, no understanding. No facts, and there is nothing to understand. The structure of knowledge is actually the conceptual structure of each discipline. So it follows that there is no understanding without both conceptual structure and facts. Skills are the tools that we use to manipulate the facts. Skills, facts, and concepts, however, are all useless unless we can do something useful with them, unless we can apply them to the myriad of complex, often ambiguous, problems that are the fabric of modern life.

Unfortunately, each of the components of a balanced curriculum has their partisans, who would advance their candidate at the expense of the others. Partisans of facts and skills would exterminate from the curriculum material that aims at conceptual understanding and applications. Partisans of understanding often think, as we just noted, that emphasizing the knowledge in each subject is a waste of time, since there is so much knowledge that it cannot possibly be covered in what will inevitably be introductory survey courses. And partisans of the "interdisciplinary" curriculum would create a curriculum more or less empty of real substance—either of the conceptual kind or the knowledge kind.

We would strongly urge you to avoid these extremes in your selection of standards, materials, and instructional methods. The ideal is the balanced curriculum, with balance defined as we have just described it. Inevitably, that will mean a curriculum that has been very carefully pruned in many different ways. We emphatically agree with Ted Sizer that "less is more," but we have in mind a modestly precise definition of "less" and "more." First, narrow the range of subjects in the curriculum to the kind of core that we described above. Second, within each subject, define with great care the core topics and concepts, being very careful to ask at each grade level, What concepts must be mastered here in order to provide the essential building blocks required for understanding the material that will be presented in subsequent grades? What skills and knowledge must be mastered in this grade that will be needed in the following grades? What assignments can be given to the students that will most effectively require them to draw on everything they have learned to solve one or more problems that are very like the problems they will encounter later on in life? Third, weld the skills, knowledge, topics, concepts and problem assignments together into a curriculum that matches the standards you have chosen.

The Safety Net Curriculum

It is not enough to say that there is a standard lower division core curriculum. What must also be said is that every student in the lower division, save only the most severely mentally handicapped, are meant to meet the standard to which that curriculum is set. So students who have problems progressing through the standard curriculum must have alternative curricula or additional curricula that will get them to the standard.

To some extent, the safety net consists of more time—before school, during the school day, after school, on Saturday mornings and during the summer. But that begs the question of what is studied during the extra time. Some of this time, perhaps much of it, should be spent in one-on-one or one-on-a-few tutoring, concentrating on basic facts and skills. There is a large literature showing that this has major positive effects on achievement, the more so when the tutoring is designed specifically to support the regular classroom instruction.

But there is also evidence to show that students who are having difficulty—and many who are not—do much better when the problems they practice on are *all* problems of an applied sort, problems that enable the student to see how the knowledge gained and the skills learned can be used to solve real-world problems. Gil Lopez, creator of one of the most effective programs for teaching mathematics to secondary students from low-income and minority backgrounds, insists on double periods for mathematics; one of the periods is used to teach the concepts and one is used to teach the applications of those concepts.

For some students, however, the regular curriculum simply will not work. These students may have given up on themselves. They might have to support their families and cannot afford to spend a full day in school. Or they might simply fail to see the connection between school and what will happen to them when they leave school. One creative superintendent gave his high school principals portable classrooms and filled them with computers to deliver software-based courses corresponding to the regular curriculum. He told the principals they could have all of the average daily attendance money for their school budget for every dropout they brought off the street and into this facility. Students could sign up for two-hour time blocks in this facility from early in the morning until late at night six days a week every week in the year. Soon they filled up with students, most of whom had full time jobs. Half of these students, all of whom had dropped out of school, ended up going on to college.

Other students will need some form of academy or theme program to catch and hold their interest. The aim here is not vocational training per se, but rather to design a program around an occupational or industrial theme that interests the student and motivates that student to stay in school and continue his or her education.

In the standards-based school, however, neither the academic program itself nor the standards on which it is based can be watered down. We are discussing alternative routes to the same goal, not a different goal. Because that is so, for example, the theme-based program might require a longer school day than the regular school program, to accommodate both the course work and the theme-related applications work. And the regular academic courses will have to be designed to constantly use illustrative examples related to the theme.

The Upper Division Curriculum

The Academic Program

Recall that the student entering the upper division has a choice between two programs: an academic program preparing the student for competitive college entrance exams and a professional and technical program preparing the student to meet industry skill standards for jobs leading to good careers. The academic program might consist of the International Baccalaureate, a program of Advanced Placement courses, or state-designed programs like the New York Regents or the Golden State Exam program in California.

The International Baccalaureate comes with complete course designs, arranged in sequences, along with materials and assessments. The Advanced Placement courses come with very good exams and course syllabi, but they do not come with their own curriculum materials nor embedded ongoing assessments. Nor are the individual courses arranged in sequences to constitute a coherent program. Thus, unless the high school picks the IB program, there is work to be done to design a coherent program from a logical sequence of courses, assemble the curriculum materials, and frame an ongoing assessment program designed to prepare the students for the examinations at the end. Many high schools will want to have more than one of these options available to their students.

Because students stay in the lower division until they have met the exit standards for the lower division (that is, they have received their CIM or its equivalent), different students will be in the upper division for different periods of time. That too, will affect the design of the upper division curriculum. Flexibility will have to be built in to allow the student, within limits, to construct a program designed to make the most of the time available to get the courses most likely to help that student reach his or her objectives, which may depend significantly on the requirements of the colleges to which that student intends to apply.

The Professional and Technical Program

The other choice the student has on entering the upper division is to choose the Professional and Technical Program. Here the student's program consists of a combination of coursework and internships in one or more workplaces, all designed to provide the skills and knowledge needed to meet an industry skill standard for a particular career or cluster of careers. In most cases, the coursework will be a combination of high school courses and courses taken in a variety of post-secondary institutions, including community colleges, technical colleges, and proprietary colleges (and, sometimes, four-year institutions).

Because, in this design, the student will have met the standards for the CIM, there will be no need for remedial courses. The student will be fully qualified for entry into freshman level community college courses whose prerequisites call for completion of 12th-grade-level work in English, mathematics, and science. Whether those courses are taken at the community college or the high school will depend on the student's preferences and the degree of technical content of the course. It is very unlikely that most high schools will be able to deliver courses with significant technical content at the required level of quality.

In time, the standards for these programs will be set by the national industry groups now starting to set standards under the auspices of the National Skill Standards Board, established by the Congress for just that purpose. At the entry level these will be standards for broad groupings of jobs that cut across industries and industry groups. The Board has adopted polices that require the standard-setting groups to specify the occupational skills and knowledge needed, the academic skills and knowledge needed, and the work-related skills and knowledge needed for each cluster of jobs and careers for which standards will be set. By "work-related skills" the Board means things such as the ability to work well as a member of a team and to take responsibility for getting a job done.

This means that they will require a new kind of curriculum. Not new in the sense that a curriculum of this kind has never existed, but new in the sense that very few educational institutions have such a curriculum in place. Even more to the point, assembling such a curriculum in today's environment means, as a practical matter, calling on the skills and capacity of a number of separate institutions to assemble a curriculum that will together be able to do the job. In time, in our view, our community and technical colleges will have to acquire the full range of capabilities needed to deliver a very high quality curriculum of the kind we are describing.

These will not be curricula with watered down academics. To the contrary, they will have strong academic content building on the work done to get the CIM and going beyond it. But the curriculum in which the academics are embedded will have to be much more applied than is typically the case in any of our secondary or postsecondary institutions.

What we have in mind is a curriculum made up of courses that are highly project-based, incorporating work in classrooms, labs, and school workshops, where the learning is driven by inquiry designed to solve a problem or build something. The expectations for what students will know as a result, about mathematics or science for example, are no less demanding than in the academic track, but the approach to that learning is far more applied or problem-focused.

As the student experiences such a curriculum, he or she will be paying attention not just to the academic requirements of the standards and the occupational skills and knowledge that he or she is gaining, but also to the work-related aspects of the standards. This will require a curriculum that is designed to enhance the kinds of characteristics we mentioned above, such as the ability to work easily with others in groups, take leadership, work independently, and so on. The trick here is not only to create a curriculum that provides opportunities to develop such skills, but also to help students develop a built-in set of metrics to judge how well they are doing about such things, and images of what good performance in such dimensions looks like.

We are uneasy leaving it at that. Building curricula that answer to this set of specifications may be one of the most interesting curriculum development challenges of the next several decades. Lurking in these few paragraphs are intricate complexities and very tough challenges. The nations that are most successful in resolving these complexities and addressing these challenges will have great advantages in the economic competition ahead.

Standards-Based Curriculum

Building high school curricula that fit the institutional structure of the new American high school was the first challenge. The second was building curricula that are based on standards. We turn now to the second challenge.

Curriculum Without Standards

The TIMSS reports put into bold relief many earlier analyses that had pointed in the same direction. Perhaps the single most important reason for the poor performance of American high school students in international comparisons of student achievement is the lack of standards in this country that could guide the construction of effective curriculum.[3]

The TIMSS study's most memorable characterization of the American curriculum is that it is "a mile wide and an inch deep." Topics important and unimportant are given the same amount of time in the curriculum, and that time is very short. So nothing is treated in depth. Nor is there a very discernible sequence. Topics are presented in helter skelter sequence. Instruction on the underlying concepts is mostly missing altogether, so students have nothing on which to hang real understanding of the topics addressed. In the place of attention to underlying concepts is a curriculum composed of activities, facts, and skills. Facts and skills are, of course, important, but without a conceptual underpinning to tie them to, they are unhinged from understanding, and therefore from the ability to apply them to unfamiliar problems. The TIMSS researchers also reported that the quality of American lessons is well below the quality of lessons in other countries, in the sense that they are not nearly as well crafted.

Taken together, this is a picture of complete disorganization. It is not that we lack curriculum courses in our teachers' colleges, curriculum supervisors in many central offices, expensive textbooks and materials, a plethora of "stuff" to facilitate a wealth of activities in the classroom, or major investment by our government in curriculum development. We have and have long had all of those things. So what is the problem?

The problem is that we have no standards.[4] In virtually every nation that has both high achievement at the top and a narrow range of achievement from top to bottom (which should be the objective of every nation), there is a clear consensus, written down and organized by the ministry of education, as to what subjects belong in the core curriculum and what topics should be taught in each of those subjects year by year. Whether the curriculum materials in those nations are developed by the government or by private enterprise, they are set to the curriculum maps issued by the ministry. Teachers all over the nation know what students coming into their classrooms should know and be able to do. They also know what they are expected to teach, and they know what their students will be examined on at the end of the year.

In this country, none of that has been true. There has been no core standard curriculum set by government at either the state or national level, subject by subject, grade by grade, topic by topic. Instead the curriculum has been set by textbook companies. To make sure that they can recover their costs, they send their sales force to teachers' committee after teachers' committee, district after district, state after state. They compile all the requests they get from all of the committees and cram the resulting list of topics and instructional methods into their specifications for the textbook writers. Little wonder that they come up with the largest and most expensive textbooks in the world!

There is far more in these textbooks than any teacher could possibly teach in a year. And far less on any one topic than is needed to really understand it in any depth. Nevertheless, our teachers take this book as if it were a syllabus, starting at the front, and attempt to teach it to their students. In this situation, most teachers rarely get beyond the middle by the end of the year, or they edit the text on the run, teaching some topics and leaving out others. Because teachers can and do edit these texts in widely varying ways, it does not pay the textbook writer to sequence the chapters in any particular way, with the result that nothing necessarily leads to anything.

Using Standards to Organize the Curriculum

So the starting point for a standards-based curriculum is to have standards that, unlike the textbook, are carefully thought through in a sequence that reflects careful selection and sequencing of topics, and the underlying concepts that go with them. The result should be a deeply pruned map of the curriculum through the grades that leaves only those topics and concepts that are truly central to the discipline, arranged in a sequence such that what happens in any given year must necessarily be mastered in order to understand what is presented in the following year. Each topic and concept that survives this pruning should be treated in depth, with the subtopics and activities carefully staged to provide an opportunity for every student to understand, use, and master the concepts involved, and thereby gain true understanding of the material.[5]

Core Assignments Linked to Standards

In a standards-based curriculum, core assignments are the task specifications for the student work linked explicitly to the standards. Core assignments are designed to help students produce work that meets standards, and to build student understanding of *what* they are expected to do, but more importantly, *why* they are doing it. The standards, along with rubrics, provide clues to the student about what is expected prior to the student's execution of the assignment. When contrasting this approach with the conventional approach of designing assignments to simply "cover material," the students are more likely to connect the work they do to the standards they are expected to meet.

A New Type of Syllabus

The link between the curriculum map and the detailed content of a particular course is the syllabus. But we have in mind a syllabus rather different from what that word may typically call to mind. The written syllabus for each course should spell out the students' academic responsibilities and the standards by which their work will be judged. This new syllabus should be common across teachers; it may be a department syllabus or a districtwide syllabus. Advanced Placement (AP) courses are good examples of how the new syllabus-based course should work.

In a standards-driven course, the role of the syllabus itself becomes quite important. As illustrated in Chapter 5, the major assignments (reading, writing, labs, and projects) for the year are described. The syllabus also lists descriptions of the student work to be produced at the end of the course—either as contained in the portfolio or as assessed on the end-of-course reference exam. The purposes of the course are also linked to the standards, which helps students to understand the broader purposes towards which their work is building. Finally, the syllabus should show the criteria of good work and point students towards examples that represent different levels of performance.

Essentially, the syllabus is a two-way commitment; it says to the student, "if you do these assignments well enough to meet these explicit standards, and you study to learn these things, you will get a good grade."

Instructional Tools That Support Student Learning

The importance of tools for professional work can be captured in a simple story. Imagine an emergency room physician returning home and reaching the scene of an automobile accident where there have been several serious injuries. She has extensive competence in dealing with these injuries, but she is caught without any of her emergency room tools. Her frustration grows as she struggles to help, but without blood plasma and instruments to stop internal bleeding, the driver of one of the vehicles involved in the accident dies before the paramedics arrive. Advanced and relevant medical competence without the tools to get her professional work done were not enough for this physician. Lawyers have and need many tools to do their jobs; so do architects, tax accountants, nurses, and others. They invest in the equipment and the training to use the tools successfully and probably couldn't perform well without the tools.

But what tools do teachers have? What tools do they need? A year-long syllabus is one type of instructional tool that helps both teachers and students by organizing teaching and learning around a set of clear standards and goals. On a day-to-day basis, however, teachers need other kinds of tools that support their instructional efforts. In a standards-driven classroom, we are picturing several types of new instructional tools:[6]

- *Concept books.* Concept books help explain some key concepts in some depth and provide prompts that help students to think about the potential applications. Because the standards for a given course will now delimit the number of key concepts to a vital few, a concept book can emphasize these vital concepts and provide a way for students to build a deep and enduring understanding of them. Concept books will be much shorter than American textbooks, bound in paperback form, and designed to be read and kept by the student.

- *Problem-solving tools.* Problem-solving tools can be in the form of science kits, historical primary source materials, problem books, and/or related tools which would help students practice and apply knowledge to a variety of settings. These tools would use ideas of applied learning to help students manage and apply their learning both within and outside a classroom. The problems posed would be supported by the appropriate cognitive scaffolding so that students were practicing using concepts they had previously learned in applications where they were able to provide powerful and interesting answers to important problems.

- *Skill-building tools.* Skill-building tools could include books, journals, technology, and other strategies for helping students build the skills they will need to meet the standards. Often, students need multiple realms of practice on increasingly demanding versions of the skills. They also need to see that the skills are important in life and are not just a function of the instruction "du jour" and an end in themselves.

Teachers will also need assessment tools that are linked to these instructional tools. These could include portfolios and reference tests within portfolios, as described in Chapter 3. And more than ever, students will need opportunities to assess their own learning by using instructional tools that reinforce the importance of reflecting on what they know as they link it to the student standards which they are working to meet.

Instructional Strategies and Interaction

Ted Sizer has given strong voice to a familiar phrase in recent high school reform: The teacher should be the coach and the student should be the knowledge worker.[7] We have added many elements to that important phrase. In the standards-based classroom, the teacher is the coach with student performance standards as the guide for student and teacher. The teacher and the student also have powerful curriculum, and tools to facilitate student learning. Next, the teacher needs to develop and use instructional strategies that help students reach the standards. *How* a teacher uses the standards, curriculum, and tools to teach classes and individual students depends on the quality of the lessons he or she designs as well as his or her own knowledge, skill, and experience.

The TIMSS study found that, in comparison with other countries, American classrooms contain very few quality lessons. Lessons typically use a considerable amount of time reviewing homework and carrying out homework for the next day. Classrooms in our high schools are often characterized by frequent interruptions from outside, as well as student interruptions, that lead to many fewer minutes devoted to instruction. But the problem goes deeper.

Many American teachers have weak strategies for helping students build conceptual understanding. The TIMSS study found that our teachers often provided only labels for concepts rather than developing a deep understanding of them. Our teachers also focused on skills and procedures in isolation rather than linking them to key concepts. Without the conceptual understanding as a base, students quickly forgot the key ideas and the skill. We should not be surprised that American teachers then need to spend so much time reteaching material year after year—on this the research is very clear.

In many ways, the individual teacher in the school is not to be blamed for this problem. Lessons in other countries were built with sustained time among a group of teachers with a clear set of student performance standards and performances in mind. Teachers in Japan, for example, were able to develop a lesson of such quality that each teacher in the group was committed to using it. The lesson was then tried out in one of the teachers' classrooms and extensively critiqued and modified before becoming available as part of the portfolio of core assignments in the school. Compare this to a beginning teacher entering a traditional American high school who is given a textbook and asked to invent lessons almost exclusively on his or her own.

So, what is a quality lesson? The main ingredient is that it helps students get to high performance levels. Some common characteristics include starting where the student is and building on strengths, using the context of the students' lives as a hook to engage them, appealing to and calling for a variety of representations, requiring students to produce both formal and practical solutions to a problem, providing built-in opportunities for refinement, and applying the subject matter to real-world experiences. Quality lessons will vary by academic discipline in important ways and have attributes that are particular to that discipline, as is illustrated in the English language arts example in the next chapter.

Of course, this could describe a quality lesson in any classroom. In a standards-based classroom, what's different is the *context* in which these lessons are developed. The lessons are not arbitrary; now they are designed around a particular purpose. A lesson is carefully thought out to build upon student understanding and produce student work that fulfills the requirements of the standards.

Quality instruction also provides opportunities for students to reflect on their work and on their progress in reaching the standards. The problem in many American high schools is that, although this reflection is an important cultural value, it isn't connected to regular teacher work. Reflection must become a central and vital part of the regular instructional process.

Explicit Criteria for Student Work

Along with common standards, and access to effective tools, each school, teacher, and student must have common expectations for the levels of student performance that will fulfill those standards. It is the crucial role of the standards to set these expectations. This is why it is so important to begin not just with content standards but with performance standards. Performance standards, as we use that term, means standards that are built around examples of actual student work that meets the standards. These samples of student work make the standards explicit, real and vivid. In a very important way, what we are telling the students is very simple: In order to meet our standards, you must produce work that looks at least as good as *this*. That is why the standards must be in place before course design can begin. Not just because the structure of the standards is the template for the curriculum map, but also because the examples of standard-meeting student work are the keystones of course and materials design.

Different standards may demand different numbers and types of student work, and a range of evidence may be necessary to demonstrate achievement for any given standard. Where the qualities necessary for a particular level of performance can be stated explicitly, a single piece of work might show that a standard has been met. Where conceptual understanding is necessary to demonstrate mastery, multiple pieces of work, which are developmental in design, may be required to show that a standard has been met. Where consistency of application becomes an important criterion for a skills-related standard, multiple pieces of work may also be required. Finally, where a standard places value on the habits of learning, such as discipline and planning, executing a task or series of tasks may be sufficient demonstration that the standard has been met.

Examples of Student Work and Rubrics

One of the most obvious and overlooked ways of helping students improve their work is to show them what high-quality work looks like. Too often, teachers' criteria for grading is a mystery to the students. When given concise and clear attributes of work that meets different levels of quality achievement, students will know what it will take to move from "C" to "B" to "A" level work. Rubrics provide a "score card" to help students understand where they are on their progress toward meeting standards. The typical rubric has several performance levels, and uses terms to describe these levels such as "basic," "proficient," and "exceeds the standard."

When concrete examples of student work are linked to a rubric or other commentary that explains what can be done to improve, students begin to build a better understanding of quality work, and how to produce it. Similarly, teachers now have core assignments and rubrics that are "grounded" with real student work to use as examples and as anchors for judging work produced by subsequent students.

Internalization of Criteria

Because curriculum and instruction in a standards-driven high school begin and end with an emphasis on student work seen against known, common, and important standards, it is essential that students know and have *internalized* the criteria for good student work.[8] Talk with Robert, a typical American student, and one finds that he knows what it takes to get a "B" in his traditional history class. He knows his teacher, sometimes by reputation alone, and what the teacher thinks is important. Robert then figures out what that teacher considers worthy of a "B" grade. He also knows what history assignments are due in the near future, but he has a hard time describing what counts as good work, or what is to be learned over the course of the year. For Robert, knowing how to obtain a "B" boils down to the social problem of pleasing the teacher.[9]

In contrast, one of this book's co-authors had an opportunity to talk with Susan, a student in England who is in the fifth form (the equivalent grade level to an American junior) about her courses. As Susan stood in her art class where student work was displayed on the walls of the classroom, she talked about the standards and criteria for good work on the project, and described a rubric for assessing a theme such as "the quality of light as it falls on objects." She also pointed out the work of three student colleagues and described how it met, to varying degrees, the standards and criteria for these projects. She then explained that these criteria would be used for the external review of the final art portfolios completed at the end of senior year in school (called the sixth form in England). She went on to describe how the criteria are used continuously in her classroom. For example, they frame the discussion and coaching between instructor and student, the self-evaluation done by Susan and her colleagues, and the decisions as to when the work is "good enough."

Susan could have been describing a process particular to art classes at the school. Instead, she was describing a schoolwide practice across curriculum subjects. She and her two colleagues demonstrated how their math class and their history class replicated the process described above. The criteria were different in some ways, and the final projects took quite different forms at the end of the sixth form, but they were practicing the essentials. There was student clarity about performance standards and expectations, and ample use of the same criteria/rubric in the daily life of the classes.

So, why would Robert and Susan be so different in their understanding and in their willingness to work hard to produce good work? One reason is that the criteria matter for high school graduation in England. Susan and her colleagues need to do well on the math, history, and art assessments to enter a university or be accepted at a technical school. In fact, performance on common, across-schools assessments is the heart of the pathway to the next levels of schooling. In contrast, Robert and his American colleagues know that their pathway to higher education is set by grade point averages, which are not linked to common standards even among teachers at the same school, and scores on the SAT, which are not linked to a given high school's curriculum in any direct way.

Another reason that Robert and Susan have a different focus on the criteria for good work has to do with the nature of instruction itself in their schools. For the new American high school to succeed in getting all students to high performance levels, many aspects of instruction in our schools will need to change, including a shift to student self-management of resources such as time, learning strategies, personal incentives, habits such as perseverance, and work production.

Public Recognition of Student Work

An emphasis on student work also includes public recognition of student work. The public display helps build pride and collective acknowledgment of the effort and the achievement, but it also has instrumental value by including what the standard and rubric are, and commentary as to why the work meets the standard. Currently, in many American schools, sports trophies rather than academic awards dominate the public display cases in the hallways and front offices. A few years ago, at a high school in Los Angeles, the school/community council was asked to send a letter of commendation to the basketball player who had just been included on an All-American list of the best 100 players in the nation. He was a wonderful player, and the school community was proud of his accomplishment. But the school also had a student who had won a Westinghouse Science Scholarship, the only student in California to win that year. The Westinghouse competition was very demanding and led to selecting 45 "All-Americans" across the country. Getting equal recognition in the trophy case for the academic All-American was a major struggle for leaders at the school, as it is in most schools. What student work is really valued in the public's eye is important for students, the school faculty, and the community.

Professional Development

Clearly, the standards-based approach to education presents enormous challenges for teachers and other staff responsible for developing and implementing curriculum and instruction. To be successful, staff must be given the support they need to fulfill their new responsibilities. This includes professional development which is focused on student needs and performance and which includes a combination of generic instructional skills as well as content-specific skills. Professional development must be ongoing and provide opportunities for staff to collaborate with colleagues and to practice the skills they learn.

Professional development began to shift a decade ago from a focus on training in workshops to a focus on a culture of continuous improvement.[10] This orientation to professional development moves us forward. But it also leaves us short of the orientation that will be needed in the new American high school.

Professional Development Implications of the New American High School

Professional development in the new American high school will occur in quite a different work context that features:

1. The CIM as a demanding and high-stakes transition accomplishment for students and high-stakes accountability mechanism for teachers at the school
2. Common student performance standards and quality performance assessment strategies linked to those standards
3. Well-designed courses of study and core assignments linked to the standards
4. Strong instruction featuring powerful program designs, new and important instructional tools, quality lessons, and student support

Each of these themes has important implications for the professional development of those working with students, especially for teachers and site administrators. Professional development in support of this instructional approach has been tried in a variety of settings, both within the United States and in other countries. From that experience, lessons can be drawn about the design and best strategies for professional development.

Implications of the CIM as a high-stakes transition accomplishment for students and a high-stakes accountability mechanism for teachers. Professional development works differently when students are focused on achieving the CIM or similar performance- and standards-based culmination certificates rather than just fulfilling seat-time requirements for graduation. Both teachers and students feel responsible for ensuring that students reach this goal. This sense of *shared accountability creates an urgency and motivation to learn* both on the part of students and on the part of faculty. Professional learning responds to a need to know, as well as an opportunity to learn.

Collective accountability also appeals to teachers' sense of fairness and engagement. When students, as well as the school, are responsible for success, teachers feel they are on a level playing field in which their professional effort and growth are matched with increased student effort. Without that sense of fairness, we have found that teachers find it difficult to justify the burden of responsibility falling on them alone. When this burden falls only on teachers, it diminishes their willingness to engage in professional growth.

Finally, *a common purpose such as the CIM creates common ground for collaboration and inquiry.* This common ground is both *within* the school as teachers and others strive to find ways to help students reach the CIM and, more importantly, *across* schools for teachers to share tools, professional insights, and strategies.

Implications of common performance standards and assessments. When individuals or school sites attempt to develop their own standards (as opposed to starting with district or state standards), extensive energy and professional development time have been given to what the standards should be, without resolving the dilemma that all teachers and students need to take these standards seriously. This has been a serious problem for professional development at the schools. In many settings, it has led to what we call "hot spots," which are parts of the school where at least a small group of teachers is using many elements of the reform.[11] The literature on professional development and school change in America overflows with insights on how to create "hot spots" in schools, but offers little insight as to how to get schoolwide, deep, and systemic change focused on clear and common student performance standards.

In our experience, the common standards give a basis for common craft knowledge. Teachers can develop this knowledge focused on standards which they know will be critical to the school's success as well as their own effectiveness. Common performance standards also give teachers critical professional tools and link their own learning to a careful analysis of the learning going on with students. As many have reported from across the country, just the act of using performance standards and tools to assess student learning has been a powerful professional development effort for teachers. Without specific performance standards, the collaborative process of professional development in schools has ended up primarily focused on process with little substantive effect on either teaching or student learning.

Implications of standards-linked courses and assignments. When curriculum at the school is focused on the CIM with a carefully orchestrated sequence of courses and core assignments, professional development moves ahead quickly. The curriculum helps to sort out which teachers are responsible for what, and provides a mechanism for coordinating curriculum across grade levels. Old approaches to coordination based on good will or vague course design have not given professional development the focus or punch that is needed.

In addition, gateway assessments give teachers a better picture of which students are prepared to engage in learning. Although students will vary in their learning approaches and needs, teachers have a better basis for honing in on quality lessons and strategies linked to specific standards. This sorting out of appropriate curriculum also helps teachers overcome problems of duplication and competition across grade levels or subjects. It provides good opportunities to find interdisciplinary connections, and to build on prior knowledge. Experience both in this country and in other countries suggests that this is a tremendous impetus to effective professional development as well.

Implications of strong instruction. An interest in strong program design is not an interest in creating teacher-proof and dumbed-down curriculum as was tried some years ago. Instead, strong program designs are the way to bring together the multiple instructional and curriculum elements needed for student performance success. These elements are a wonderful strategy for synthesizing research in best practices and making it easily available for teacher use. When this happens, teacher professional development can be sophisticated and powerful. It helps teachers learn and adapt the program design to work best in their schools. It also provides them with tools that must be understood and mastered. It gets to the heart of good professionalism.

Good program design also builds opportunities for reflection, training, and tools to be linked together as professional development. Teachers need collaborative planning and inquiry, but we have found that this is best done when linked with tools, program design, and a substantive focus on specific student performance indicators and results.

Two New Approaches to Professional Development

These themes and their implications for professional development point to two promising strategies for carrying out professional development: professional development networks linked to subject matter and student performance, and within-school lesson study groups.

Professional development networks linked to subject matter and student performance. The good news is that, in recent years, professional development networks have been an important and popular strategy for teacher professional growth.[12] At best, these networks provide leadership collaboration and new insights for professional practice at a given school, and often assist individual teachers in their professional growth. The bad news is that these networks less frequently have a sustained impact on teachers' classroom practice. More importantly, the professional development networks rarely have had an impact beyond the participation of the individual teacher.

Professional development networks linked to subject matter and student performance have quite a different opportunity for success. First, they link teachers who are working in a similar subject area towards helping students reach the same or very similar student performance success. Teachers in this setting not only have more accountability for student success, they have better tools for assessing that success and providing instruction through strong program designs, instructional tools, quality lessons, and student support. They can also gauge the success of their professional development by looking at the impact on student performance. In the state of Victoria, Australia, this has given the networks more vitality and more focus.

Lesson study groups. An analysis of lessons from the videotape portion of the TIMSS study showed the power of a team of teachers at a school who were focused on the same student performance results.[13] These teachers collaborated to build quality lessons, tried them out and critiqued them, and then had them available for their common use as part of the regular school practice. These lesson study groups have focused extensively on building conceptual understanding among students and have led to lessons in those countries being especially strong by an international analysis of instructional effectiveness. We think such lesson study groups would be especially helpful in the new American high school.

Summary

The new structure of the new American high school requires new thinking about an appropriate standard core curriculum for the lower division that enables every student to master the standard for admission to the upper division program. The same can be said for the two upper division programs, one a demanding academic program preparing students for competitive college entrance examinations and the other for an equally demanding program intended to prepare students to meet the new industry skill standards and for a lifetime of continued formal education.

A standards-based orientation requires new ways of thinking about curriculum and instruction which will require a considerable amount of time, energy, and support to implement. But just look at the professional tool kit that teachers would have in the new American high school:

- Standards and standards-linked assessments both at the system and classroom levels
- Core assignments
- Exemplars of student work
- A course design linked to standards
- Powerful instructional programs
- New instructional tools like concept, problem-solving, and skill-building books and kits

In the end, though, it is not the tool kit that is important. It is what that tool kit makes possible—a curriculum designed to make sure that no one falls through the cracks, that almost every student will get a diploma, a diploma that signifies that the person who earned it has what it takes to go to college and succeed there. That is a powerful curriculum, a curriculum to bring the high school's promise up to date, a curriculum well worth fighting for.

Notes

1. The notion of a well-articulated sequence or progression is quite different from the traditional spiral curriculum. Schmidt et al. (1996) found that spiral curricula in the American context often amounted to redundancy and disorganization of curriculum across grade levels. The spiral became the merry-go-round where the same material was revisited time and time again. McDonald (1996),

Schlechty (1997), and Newmann and Associates (1996) have discussed the concept of planning backwards to help all students reach high student achievement. The National Center on Education and the Economy has developed a set of strategies for helping schools design their school environment linked to the New Standards Student Performance Standards.

2. The concept of a superficial curriculum is discussed extensively in Schmidt et al. (1996) and Newmann and Associates (1996). The Coalition of Essential Schools has also focused on depth over coverage using the aphorism, "less is more." Muncey and McQuillan (1996) have analyzed schools participating in the Coalition of Essential Schools and have identified dilemmas in getting this depth established at school sites.

3. The TIMSS study was designed based on a multifaceted and multi-layered curriculum framework (Schmidt, McKnight, & Raizen, 1997) to collect data on student achievement in 41 countries from three aspects: *content, performance expectation,* and *perspectives* of the curricula, instructional practices, school, and social factors. The study involved students and teachers from primary (grades 3-4), middle (grades 7-8), and high (grade 12) schools. The results of middle school student achievement were released in November 1996 and the results from the primary level came out in June 1997 (Beaton, Martin, Mullis, Gonzalez, Smith, & Kelly, 1996a; 1996b; 1997a; 1997b). Educators can use the findings and information to define a "world-class" education by carefully examining educational policy and practices (Peak, 1996) through the prism of other countries.

Schmidt et al. (1996) compared the pedagogical characteristics among six countries—France, Japan, Norway, Spain, Switzerland, and the United States—to develop curriculum instruments for the TIMSS, and the major assumption they made is that "teaching is fundamentally embedded in culture—both in its conception and execution" (p. 2). The critical impacts of what should be taught on teaching have shed light on our thinking in curriculum-related policy making. Schmidt, McKnight, and Raizen (1997) point out how the unfocused education in the United States detrimentally affects teachers' daily practices and students' performance. In addition, TIMSS video study of mathematics instruction in Germany, Japan, and the United States (Stigler & Hiebert, 1997) has also shown solid information about the processes of teaching and learning inside the U.S. classrooms and crucial information for developing sound education policy. Stigler and Hiebert concluded that the importance of setting educational goals can lead teacher preparation to focus on the direct study of teaching high-quality and thinking-oriented lessons.

4. Both England and the State of Victoria in Australia have developed common standards across the nation or state. They have also developed levels of student performance (called Key Stages in England and Key Learning Areas in Victoria). These have greatly facilitated the analysis of student performance that informs instructional improvement. In contrast, standards-driven reform in the United States has been characterized by standards and performance indexes with data that are less useful for instructional improvement (the Kentucky example, see Kentucky Department of Education, 1995) or local school inspection of student work. This local inspection of student work, however, has often had fuzzy and rapidly changing standards so that the instructional improvement was difficult to realize.

5. The importance of clear criteria and the way to make these a living reality in the school has been discussed in several recent reform efforts by McDonald (1996), Schlechty (1997), and Darling-Hammond (1997). A further discussion of different kinds of standards and how to make them clear to students, with examples of student work, is found in the New Standards Performance Standards Volume 3—high school.

6. These instructional tools are discussed further in Tucker and Codding (1998). Our collective thinking has been deeply influenced by the experience in several Asian countries, as documented in the TIMSS study as found in Schmidt, et al. (1996) and Stigler and Hiebert (1997).

7. The idea of teacher as coach and student as knowledge worker is explained further by Sizer in Sizer (1985), Sizer (1992), and Sizer (1996).

8. For further analysis of student engagement in meeting high standards, see McDonald (1996) for a discussion of the tuning protocol and student engagement. Wasley, et al. (1997) describes student attitudes toward getting engaged and Newmann and Associates (1996) provides a comprehensive view of the relationship of curriculum and instruction to student engagement and the standards.

9. McDonald (1996) discusses a tuning protocol that helps teachers and students to create greater understanding and internalization of criteria and rubrics for their work. Wasley, et al. (1997) talks about the difficulty of getting rigor and standards established at the school level. The New Standards Performance Standards produced by the National Center on Education and the Economy and discussed in *Performance Standards, Volume 3, High School: English Language Arts,*

Mathematics, Science, Applied Learning (1997) includes examples of student work and contains a powerful strategy for focusing on student work in school settings.

10. The shift from a focus on training in workshops to a focus on a culture of continuous improvement has been discussed creatively and extensively by Little (1993) and Fullan (1993) in what is perhaps the most influential book concerning educational change, *Change Forces*. The more specific analysis of the shift from training to culture is provided in Sparks and Hirsh (1997).

11. The concept of hot spots was originated by Marsh and Crocker (1991) in a study of middle school reform in California. Eight exemplary middle schools were identified that were thought to be quite advanced in their use of components of the state task force report on middle schools, *Caught in the Middle*. All eight middle schools were found to have serious intentions to implement these reform elements, but the extent of implementation was only moderate across the schools, but the moderate rating masked the internal diversity within the school. Some classrooms in the school reflected extensive use of *Caught in the Middle* elements, while others reflected essentially no implementation at all.

12. Professional development networks have been an important strategy for teacher professional growth. Lieberman and McLaughlin (1992) identified key features of successful networks. However, they also reported that networks typically led to change for the individual teacher, but did not transform the school. Lieberman and Grolnick (1997) have extended the idea of teacher networks and provided more examples of key elements.

13. Stigler reports that lesson study groups have been highly effective in the Japanese setting. He describes the national focus on student performance and how teachers at the school have internalized this standards-based focus. With that as context, groups of teachers within a school have developed lessons linked to this view of standards. Teachers typically developed the lessons as a group, and one member then tried out the lesson, which was then critiqued by the group. After subsequent revisions, the lessons were used by all teachers in the lesson study group. Annual exchanges of lessons among study groups has led to wide, teacher-centered distribution and use of these quality lessons. Stigler and Hiebert (1997) and Schmidt, et al. (1996) give ample evidence to the quality of lessons used in Japan as contrasted with the marginal quality of lessons used in the United States.

5

Standards-Based
Classrooms in High Schools
An Illustration

Sally Hampton

AS DISCUSSED IN Chapters 3, "Standards and Assessment," and 4, "Rethinking Curriculum and Instruction," a successful classroom in the new American high school is based on clearly defined standards that lead to the achievement of a Certificate of Initial Mastery (CIM). Criteria for student work, courses, core assignments, lessons, instructional methodology, instructional tools, student assessments, and professional development all support students' achievement of those standards. Of course, this is easier said than done. When all these pieces are put together, what does the new standards-based classroom really look like? How can teachers implement an instructional program that is focused on a coherent vision and ensures that students perform to high expectations?

This chapter presents an illustration of such a classroom. It uses the English language arts standards framework in New Standards (1997) as the basis for the instructional program, but the ideas could be applied to any state- or district-designed standards framework.[1] Those standards are the starting point for classroom practice—they are, in fact, what all students in the class are responsible for knowing and being able to do. The standards, syllabus, and portfolio are the organizing features of the standards-based classroom, so it is important that students recognize their relationship to one another. Instruction in standards-based classrooms is tied directly to the standards and provides multiple opportunities for students to produce work that meets the standards.

Overview of the Standards-Based Classroom

When you first walk through the door, the standards-based classroom may not appear much different from any other classroom. But look closer. Something special is happening here.

In an ideal standards-based classroom, there are no secrets about students' academic responsibilities. The standards are posted on the walls of the classroom, as are rubrics showing the criteria for judging student work and examples of student work that meets those standards. Early in the school year, these examples of student work may be from the previous year so that incoming students understand the level of work that will be expected of them. In our hypothetical English class, these examples include poems written by students, entries from a dialogue journal that compare two or more stories in theme or characterization, and critiques of a political speech developed during a social studies class.

The teacher spends time reviewing the standards at the beginning of the year and explains that these standards represent course goals. He or she presents the syllabus for the year that spells out the students' assignments related to those standards. In addition to or instead of posting the standards on the wall, the teacher may include in the syllabus or in a separate document a summary of the standards along with commentary about how the core assignments relate to the standards.

The teacher reinforces the standards by sending to parents or guardians a letter that explains the standards. Parents are aware of the higher expectations for students, and understand that many standards require an increased amount of reading or other homework and a greater responsibility on the part of students to take charge of their own learning and performance.

Grading and assessment practices are no longer a mystery to students and their parents. Instead of being graded on the content of written assignments in one classroom, grammar in another, and classroom participation in yet another, students must meet criteria that match the standards and reflect the course of study laid out in the syllabus. Students spend time studying examples of student work that fulfill the requirements, and may review the work of others as a way to help in their own understanding of the criteria. They have internalized the standards and can describe the criteria for student work, and they understand that they need to fulfill these requirements to obtain the CIM, which holds the key to future opportunities.

Assessments are varied to allow students to demonstrate their proficiency in a variety of ways; they may include some oral discussion, some written work that students have had an opportunity to revise, and some on-demand tasks. As part of the assessment system, the classroom contains portfolios in which students can collect and store their best work throughout the year. These portfolios are organized into exhibits, each focusing on a particular area of performance (e.g., reading) and consisting of one or more entries. "Entry slips" tell students exactly what is required and how it will be assessed. A cover page sets out the task, circumstances of performance, and standards to which the task is related. The teacher explains the options within the portfolio system and makes explicit how the portfolio ties into the performance standards.

The emphasis on standards and standards-based assessments extends to the rest of the educational program as well. For example, the content of the curriculum appears more structured. There is coherence from grade level to grade level so that students can build on previously learned skills. Assignments gain in complexity but remain focused on the standards. Textbooks are "pruned" of supplementary activities that do not enable students to reach the standards. The instructional strategies and methodologies used to deliver the curriculum continue to reflect the individual styles of teachers but are focused on the common goals.

The physical arrangement of desks and equipment varies from classroom to classroom but is designed to support the work being done. This may mean a more flexible arrangement of desks that provides enough space for the teacher to move between desks and allows students to move their desks to work in teams or to find a quieter place for reading. The classroom may contain lots of books that students can access whenever they have finished a project and have some time for reading.

In short, what is different about the standards-based classroom is a clear sense that teaching and learning are focused on a vision of what students need to know and be able to do. Standards, assessment, and assignments do not feel arbitrary or capricious. Everyone is working together to maximize student achievement.

Using English Language Arts Standards to Plan Assignments

How does a teacher actually develop a course and day-to-day lessons focused on a set of standards? At first, he or she will probably be overwhelmed by a comprehensive standards framework. The New Standards (1997) framework in English language arts is no exception. The seven standards for high schools address the following:

1. Reading
2. Writing
3. Speaking, listening, and viewing
4. Conventions, grammar, and use of language
5. Literature
6. Public documents
7. Functional documents

To meet these standards, there is much work to be done: 25 books, 6 kinds of writing, 2 kinds of oral reports, 4 kinds of literature, and public and functional documents. With ample planning, however, the standards are not so daunting. Teachers should plan most assignments by working backward from the target standard to the kinds of activities the students need to experience to produce work of appropriate quality. In addition, even though English teachers may accept primary responsibility for English language arts standards, teachers across the curriculum should share responsibility for the related assignments. This provides opportunities for students to meet the standards in a variety of ways and to use some activities to fulfill standards in more than one subject matter (e.g., a report produced in a science class may also count toward the writing standard).

Let's take a closer look at the standards for reading, writing, and speaking, listening, and viewing to see how the teacher in our standards-based English class might develop assignments that help students achieve these standards.

Reading

Among the reading standards is a requirement that students read 25 books or "book equivalents" each year. This is a different kind of standard in that it is focused on quantity (how many) rather than quality of work or level of understanding, but New Standards (1997) based this reading standard on research that shows that reading is a skill improved only through practice and that an extensive amount of reading builds vocabulary, writing, and other skills. For these reasons, the number of books students are expected to read each year remains the same throughout each grade level; of course, the complexity of the material increases along with the skill level.

One of the first decisions that needs to be made involves identifying the types of reading materials that will count toward this 25-book requirement. Reading materials should include traditional and contemporary literature (both fiction and nonfiction) as well as magazines, newspapers, textbooks, and on-line materials. In fact, New Standards (1997) requires that students read a diverse set of materials representing at least three different literary forms and at least five different writers.

A sample reading list is available in New Standards (1997) to demonstrate the quality and complexity of the materials to be read at the high school level. It includes works of fiction such as *Alice in Wonderland* (Carroll, 1832) and *Lord of the Flies* (Golding, 1911); nonfiction such as John F. Kennedy's (1956) *Profiles in Courage;* poetry; drama; folklore and mythology; modern fantasy and science fiction; magazines; newspapers; and materials such as computer or technical manuals. Other lists are produced by such organizations as the National Council of Teachers of English and the American Library Association, or are developed locally.

The teacher provides students with a suggested reading list and gives students some rough guidelines about the term *book equiva-*

lents—for example, that 200 pages of high school level material equals a book. She reminds students that if they are required to read a book for their history class or science class, that book counts toward the 25-book requirement. Because the school year is approximately 36 weeks, students should know that they need to read roughly 150 pages per week if the reading standard is to be accomplished during the school year alone. Of course, much of what students have to read can be done outside of school—even over the summer months.

Students' access to reading materials must be considered. Our teacher knows that the resources at the school library are inadequate to support the amount of reading required for every student to achieve this standard, and she is prepared to help students locate appropriate materials through local or county libraries or other community resources.

Because students will fulfill the reading standard in a variety of ways and across a number of classrooms and settings, coordination among teachers at the high school will be necessary to establish whether an individual student has met the standard. Decisions need to be made about the reporting mechanisms. What activities will provide evidence of reading 25 books? Will students maintain an annotated list of works read, generate a reading log or journal, or participate in formal and informal book talks?

In our example, the teacher provides students with a sample reading report log in which students will document their reading. Reading logs are structured in a variety of ways, but their essential purpose is to provide students with the opportunity to record impressions of the text; summarize what has been read; make connections between sections of the text, among texts, or between text and personal knowledge; puzzle through the complexities of the text; and comment on stylistic features.

To become confident about the reading load, students keep a reading diary for several weeks and catalogue all the reading they do. The teacher suggests that they set the goal of reading at least 30 minutes each school night in addition to doing their other assignments. To encourage students to meet the 25-book standard, the teacher reminds students that there is a correlation between reading and high SAT scores. End-of-course exams also provide motivation and make the work more relevant.

Writing

The teacher in our hypothetical classroom finds that her students are often unprepared for the rigor of the writing curriculum and that she will need to develop plans to get these students on track to do the work expected of them. Such planning is best undertaken when teachers at adjacent grade levels decide to work together (grades 9 and 10 would be ideal) to give students adequate time to become proficient in terms of the writing standard.

For example, at grade 10 in the New Standards design, students must demonstrate proficiency in six genres:

1. Report writing
2. Response to literature
3. Narrative account
4. Narrative procedure
5. Persuasive essay
6. Reflective essay

For students who come to high school with little experience or instruction in writing, the standards may take 2 or 3 years to achieve. It makes good sense for the 9th-grade teacher to assume responsibility for part of the standards requirements. In our hypothetical school, the teacher in grade 9 addresses the report, the response to literature, and the narrative account; the teacher in grade 10 maintains these and teaches, in addition, the narrative procedure, the persuasive essay, and the reflective essay. In both cases, the teacher determines one genre with which to begin and then designs a series of lessons to teach students about writing that genre.

The teacher designs an assignment sequence that fits into the curriculum and develops important writing strategies for students, ensuring that the assignment series has the following elements:

1. The criteria necessary to succeed (rubrics) are taught directly to students. Over the course of the year, these rubrics change in two ways: The papers that represent score points become increasingly proficient, and the elements of each score point become more demanding.

2. The students have multiple opportunities to write short pieces to practice specific parts of genres, such as interesting beginnings or personas.

3. The assignments and the content gain in complexity.

4. The students produce one or more final products that incorporate all genre features successfully.

5. The students have some choice and independence in topic selection and are given alternative methods to produce a successful piece. This gives students multiple opportunities to develop proficiency in any particular genre, and to distinguish between their various efforts and make a wise choice about which writing effort is the most successful. Making such choices about quality forces students to evaluate their work vigorously and to come to terms with their strengths and weaknesses as writers.

6. Models of competent student work and adult performance are accessible for students to analyze. So, for example, there are editorials that exemplify good persuasive writing and brochures that are good representations of informational writing. The teacher includes some of these samples as attachments to the syllabus.

In our classroom, the curriculum begins with a unit on poetry, so the first assignment has students reading two poems, deciding what the poems mean to them, and then telling which poem they like better and why. This is an assignment that requires a writer to compare and evaluate. The teacher may use this assignment whenever she wants students to develop writing around evaluation and analysis. That is, it works regardless of which poems the teacher assigns and, in fact, it is an assignment that works if students consider two characters in a novel, two short stories, or two historical periods. The teacher focuses on how well the student is able to shape writing that compares two things and how well the student supports an evaluative judgment.

The same assignment might be given at the start of both grades 9 and 10—in grade 9 to introduce this particular form of writing and in grade 10 to revisit and refine skills the students developed the previous year. It is an assignment that may grow in complexity as students first compare and evaluate things with which they are familiar (poems studied in class) and then move to things with which they are unfamiliar (unstudied poems, short stories, or contemporary issues requiring some research). Or the complexity may be built into the difficulty of the two things being written about—moving from, say, two Emily Dickinson poems to two more complex pieces by Frost to still more complex pieces by Eliot. Although the teacher builds increasing complexity into the assignments, the students are also expected to meet increasingly rigorous criteria.

The English teacher takes primary responsibility for teaching the writing standard. Work done in classes other than English is a source for portfolio entries, however. A student may produce a narrative procedure in science or computer science class or a report in social studies or health.

Another way the teacher provides choices to students is by requiring certain readings but allowing students to choose the mode of writing that grows out of the readings. So, for example, after the class has read John Knowles's *A Separate Peace*, students may produce any of the following:

- A report on several books, all of which focus on the boarding school experience
- A response to literature that analyzes the text as a rite-of-passage novel
- A narrative account that juxtaposes the experiences of Gene with that of the student author's recounting of the first year of high school
- A narrative procedure that lays out the rules for "playing" Finney's game
- A persuasive essay that argues for rituals of initiation (the jump from the tree)
- A reflective essay that uses the conflict in the book as a microcosm for both human conflict and male bonding

Speaking, Listening, and Viewing

New Standards (1997) defines speaking, listening, and viewing as fundamental processes that people use to express, explore, and learn about new ideas. They include gathering and sharing information; persuading others; expressing and understanding ideas; coordinating activities with others; and selecting and critically analyzing messages.

These communications may take place in the context of one-to-one conferences, small-group interactions, large audiences and meetings, or interactions with broadcast media.

One specific standard requires students to prepare and deliver an individual presentation. To help students meet this standard, the teacher spends time brainstorming with students about possible activities. Examples include:

- An individual talk that develops several main points relating to a single thesis (e.g., describing a problem and evaluating alternative solutions to that problem, explaining several causes leading to a historical event, or constructing different types of arguments, all supporting a particular policy)
- A public panel discussion during which each member of the panel speaks about a particular area of expertise relating to the overall topic
- A forum discussion during which audience members question and respond to panelists during the presentation
- A simulated congress (e.g., Model United Nations) in which each participant "represents" the interests of a particular constituency

Often students recognize only the English class as the source for work in the English language arts portfolio. They fail to realize how much they routinely do that could count toward meeting the standards. So the teacher talks students through the examples from the New Standards (1997) book. She ensures that students understand that any presentation they do in school or out of school may count as a performance in speaking. Some students are in church, scouting, or other community groups that allow them to make oral presentations. Vocational and fine arts classes also require oral presentations from time to time. And many students take a speech course, which obviously provides multiple occasions for performance.

At the same time, these types of presentations may fulfill other standards as well, including those related to conventions, grammar, and use of the English language; writing a persuasive essay; or reading informational materials and incorporating those materials into a speech.

Putting It All Together in a Syllabus

As described in Chapter 4, "Rethinking Curriculum and Instruction in the New American High School," the course syllabus is both a road map and a time line. It maps out the terrain to be traveled and establishes checkpoints that determine if students are keeping up.

The design of a syllabus that leads students to the English language arts standards is a departmental responsibility. An English department will, for example, need to determine which genres should be taught at which grade levels, and how to sequence assignments to ensure that student proficiency in writing increases along with the complexity of the content being written about. Of course, there will be wide latitude as to the specificity of any particular assignment, but there should be a core of expected readings and genre assignments that guarantees that students will be able to meet the standards.

Because some students new to standards will take more than 1 year to meet all the English language arts standards, a 2-year plan is the first step in designing a syllabus. If three types of the required six genres of writing are addressed in year 1, and if students also begin to read on a routine basis and log their reading entries during this time, then a syllabus for year 2 (presumably grade 10) would require that students do the following, at a minimum:

1. Read three to five books as part of the literature curriculum. (These should be pivotal pieces that serve as the basis for discussing other work.)

2. Complete four writing assignments, three of which are mandatory requirements and one that is optional. For example, the assignment might read:

   Complete each of the following:
   - One response to literature, functional writing, or technical writing
   - One persuasive essay
   - One reflective essay

   Then, choose one of the following:
   - One narrative account
   - One narrative procedure
   - One report of information

3. Read and critique selections chosen from a literature anthology.

4. Read and critique some functional documents.

5. Read and critique some public documents.

6. Produce at least two oral reports.

Let's consider specifically one curriculum design for grade 10. Assume that the curriculum is built around a study of literary forms or types. The syllabus for that year would include the elements identified in Chapter 4, including a summary of the standards, a description of the core assignments, and a few samples of student work along with a rubric. A portion of the syllabus for the fall semester identifying core assignments might look like Figure 5.1.

Evaluating Student Work

The students in our English class are working on the assignments specified in the course syllabus and are looking across all their courses to ensure that they fulfill the standards that lead to the CIM. But how will they know when their performance on any given standard has reached acceptable levels? In the standards-based classroom, assessment criteria are clear and there will be no doubts.

Standards-Based Assessment

Early in the school year, the teacher in the standards-based classroom separates assessment of standards from grading. The standards represent very high levels of performance toward which students are working. The teacher expects all students to work toward meeting these standards and to assemble work samples in the portfolio as evidence of progress and effort. The rubric is used for diagnostic purposes and supports the students' expanding understanding of the criteria of what counts as good work.

Standards-based assessments indicate whether the student meets the standard or has not yet met the standards. These designations are important because they make explicit the expectation that all will eventually succeed. At the end of each grading period, students do a

First Semester

September-October   *Short Stories*

1. Read and discuss selections from literature anthology.
2. Maintain reading log and daily dialogue journal with the following required entries:
   - 3 entries that compare two or more stories in theme or characterization;
   - 1 entry that compares the role of setting in two stories;
   - 1 entry that evaluates realistic elements of characterization and setting in one story;
   - 1 entry that evaluates narrative point of view in one story; specifically consider perspective/voice of the narrator; and
   - 1 entry that evaluates appropriateness of word choice to characterization.
3. Read *A Separate Peace* outside of class. Keep a dialogue journal that focuses on:
   - realistic elements of characterization;
   - the perspective/voice of the narrator; and
   - the choice of words used to describe character.
4. Core assignments:
   - October 25: Turn in work from short story journal that is appropriate evidence of the literature standard for portfolio.
   - November 1: Evaluative essay: Choose one short story you have read and evaluate its worth relative to setting, character, and narrative point of view.

October 26-November 30

1. Class discussion: *A Separate Peace*.

Figure 5.1. Excerpt from a Syllabus: English Language Arts, Grade 10
NOTE: In addition to the listed assignments, the syllabus would include the standards for student performance and the rubrics for each of the genres of writing for the year. Students would also have access to writing samples that meet and don't meet the standard, as well as to commentary about the samples vis-à-vis the rubric.

2. Core assignments: Each Friday a short paper is due on one of the following topics related to *A Separate Peace*: character/setting/realism/personal connections/rite of passage.

3. Read outside of class *The Loneliness of the Long Distance Runner*. Maintain dialogue journal with the same focus as the short story journal.

December 1-5

1. In class: Group the five papers on *A Separate Peace* into a major literary response paper and work with response groups to determine focus and stances.

December 7

1. Major paper #2 (drawn from work done December 1-5): a response to literature based on *A Separate Peace*.

2. Core assignments:
   - December 15: Dialogue journal from homework novel.
   - December 20: Major paper #3 "A Major Theme Running Through Certain Genres is the Rite of Passage."

Second Semester

Work during the second half of the year will address the following:

Readings
   - Functional discourse
   - Public discourse
   - Poetry
   - Essays

Assignments
   - 3 major papers
   - Dialogue journals
   - Selected short writings (miniessays/personal reflections)
   - Poetry

Figure 5.1. *(Continued)*

NOTE: The syllabus might also list a summary of the topics to be covered in Semester 2 to help students understand how their work fits into a bigger picture.

self-assessment to determine where they are in relation to the standards and which standards they still need to work on. The portfolio exhibits provide the context for this—which entries are ready, which ones still need revision, which ones have no work ready at all. At the end of the year, when the portfolio is complete, the portfolio is assessed and the students get the scoring form back as feedback.

Evaluation of Student Work: An Illustration

Figure 5.2 shows how a student's written assignment can be used to measure his or her ability to meet two different English language arts standards. The student produced a descriptive essay intended to fulfill both the writing standard for producing a narrative procedure and the conventions, grammar, and use of the English language standard for demonstrating an understanding of the rules of the English language.

To validate the claim that this essay represents standards-quality work, a student or teacher evaluating the work must "unpack" it in very specific terms. The evaluator must consider each criterion related to these two standards. For example, the evaluator has to consider persona, context, and strategies for developing reader interest. The evaluator should be able to appreciate that the writer has used these elements at an acceptable level of quality in the essay, and should show how specific text elements do or do not meet the criteria.

In Figure 5.2, the task, circumstances of performance, and related standards are first set out to remind the evaluator of the purposes and criteria of the assignment. The student work follows, with the evaluator's commentary presented in column 2 and linked to specific text elements in column 1.

Peer Support

It is helpful if, several times each grading period, students engage in a 15- to 20-minute period to "take stock." The teacher posts the work that has been assigned and evaluated; then students, working in teams, check with each other to make sure that each team member is caught up. When a student is not doing the work, the student confers with other team members for ideas about how to make up work and then writes the teacher a memo of explanation.

The task:

The student was asked to describe a narrative procedure.

Circumstances of performance:

This sample of student work was produced under the following conditions:

- Alone
- As homework
- Opportunity for revision

Standards to which the work is related:

This assignment reflects two English language arts standards: 1) a writing standard for producing a narrative procedure, and 2) a conventions, grammar, and usage of the English language standard for demonstrating an understanding of the rules of the English language.

The writing standard requires the student to produce a narrative procedure that:

- Engages the reader by establishing a context, creating a persona, and otherwise developing reader interest
- Provides a guide to action for a complicated procedure in order to anticipate a reader's needs; creates expectations through predictable structures (e.g., headings); and provides smooth transitions between steps
- Makes use of appropriate writing strategies, such as creating a visual hierarchy and using white space and graphics as appropriate
- Includes relevant information
- Excludes extraneous information

Figure 5.2. Student Work Sample: Blue-Gray Eyes

NOTE: This work sample and commentary are based on an example from New Standards (1997). Highlighting of various sections of the text and the overall analysis were added by the chapter author.

- Anticipates problems, mistakes and misunderstandings that might arise for the reader
- Provides a sense of closure to the writing

The conventions standard requires that the student independently and habitually demonstrates an understanding of the rules of the English language in written and oral work, and selects the structures and features of language appropriate to the purpose, audience, and context of the work. The student must demonstrate control of:

- Grammar
- Paragraph structure
- Punctuation
- Sentence construction
- Spelling
- Usage

Overall analysis:

Italics and boxes were added to the following student writing sample to point out key elements. The italicized text is actually the frame or backbone on which this narrative procedure hangs. The boxed words and phrases are the transition elements that chronologically link the various stages in the recounting of the procedure. There is sufficient detail but really no extraneous detail—except perhaps that which is scattered throughout the writing to provide the reader with a sense of the writer's persona.

Although a reader would love to read past the document's nontraditional elements (the song lyrics and the opening context-setting remarks), this writing does lay out the steps in a procedure and the directions could be followed if one were so inclined (though maybe only by a person whose general disposition aligns with that of the writer).

Figure 5.2. *(Continued)*

Student writing sample:

" . . . Blue-gray eyes . . . they change with the color . . . , Change with the sun . . . they run with the sight, They change with the wind . . . but they're always bright, Bright eyes . . . Blue Denim, Bright eyes . . . Blue Denim . . . "   **A**

The chorus to "Blue Denim," a song off Stevie Nicks' CD Street Angel, blares for probably the twenty-fifth time from my CD player. I'm singing right along, having the whole CD memorized by now, along with 10,000 Maniac's *Our Time in Eden,* Enya's *Watermark,* and Diana Ross & The Supremes, all of which I've been listening to almost constantly since they arrived in the mail from BMG. At the moment I'm putting on the finishing touches to the paint on the loft walls of my room, and I look like I just walked out of a paint ball war in — **J** which the other team had a smashing victory using slightly peachish-white paint (though this is nothing compared to what I looked like during the texturing stage).   — **C**

The very first step in finishing the walls in my room was to pack up all my stuff and move — **E** it out. Hah! Easier said than done. I am a pack rat. I love to sort and organize and derive great pleasure from getting rid of things, but it doesn't happen very often. Once everything was neatly packed into boxes and set in safe, semi-out-of-the-way places, my dad came in to put up the sheet rock. When it was up, the whole thing was my baby.

I spent about a day caulking the walls. The sheet rock had been hard to put up because the board behind it couldn't always be found on the first bang of the hammer, so there were lots of extra dents to be filled with putty. Dabbing a bit of putty, smoothing it over, dabbing a bit of putty, smoothing it over. Then there were the corners (my favorite), and the seams that had to be covered with tape and smoothed over with putty . . .

Commentary

A. The student created a thoroughly enjoyable persona by employing two different types of language—popular music lyrics and a narrative about painting a room—in a way that non-linear procedure becomes literary.

B. The reader's interest is engaged by the use of lyrics from popular songs to organize the essay and to reflect an attitude toward the procedure.

C. A clear guide for a complicated procedure is provided through the use of smooth transitions between steps.

Figure 5.2. *(Continued)*

Student writing sample:		Commentary
"You win a prize for that, for telling lies like — **B** *that so well that I believed it. I never felt cheated. You were the chosen one, the pure eyes of Noah's dove. Choir boys and angles [angels] stole your lips and your halo . . . " ("Noah's Dove"—10,000 Maniacs)*		**D.** The student provided a clear sense of closure by reflecting on the experience and by ending with lyrics that are appropriate to the reflection.
Once all the walls were caulked, they had to be textured. I sat on the flour [floor], which —**H** was covered in plastic drop cloths, and experimented with different textures and techniques on an extra piece of sheet rock. I decided to go with an original design of my own that consisted of interweaving rainbow-shaped strokes made with a small hand broom. I mixed up a bunch of plaster with just the right consistency (it was different every time) and got —**F** to work. I spent hours sitting on the flour [floor] making strokes with the broom, standing —**K** making strokes with the broom, balancing on the ladder making strokes with the broom, and stooping in my loft making strokes with the broom. Every once in a while there would be some bugs, cobwebs, or dried bits of plaster that would get stuck in a stroke, and I'd have to pick them out and redo it. Whenever I got plaster somewhere it wasn't supposed to be, I just wiped it off on myself. I could be washed. Between mixing plaster and wiping things off, I was soon covered. It was all over my shirt, shorts, legs, arms, hands, feet, tools, and there —**G** was even a little bit in my hair. Nobody could deny that I had been deeply involved in my task. After two or three days of texturing, I was finally done . . .		The work displays a controlled, sophisticated group of sentence structure including:
		E. The effective use of fragments;
		F. Parenthetical comments; and
		G. Effective repetitive elements.
		H. The student made two spelling mistakes which may have been merely a typographical error ("flour" instead of "floor").
"For love, forget me, I didn't mean for him to get me. Get up in the morning, and I'm filled with desire. No, no I can't stop the fire, love is a real live fire. Love is a burning sensation, far beyond imagination. Love is like an itching in my heart, tearing it all apart, an itching in my heart, and baby I can't scratch it . . . " ("Love Is Like An Itching In My Heart"—Diana Ross & The Supremes)		**I.** This error in usage does not detract from

Figure 5.2. *(Continued)*

Student writing sample:	Commentary
Then I started the painting. First, there was the coat of white primer, which thankfully didn't take very long. Then there were the two coats of slightly peach tinted white paint (you know, one of those twenty-five new shades of white), which I managed to slop all over the drop cloths and myself. We have this great roller with a long handle that I got to use, and attempt ──I to maneuver when that nice long handle was hitting some large space occupying object, such as a bookshelf or desk. "I will not become ──L frustrated. I will not become frustrated . . . " I had to wait in between coats for the paint to dry and spent a few wonderful nights sleeping on the couch so I wouldn't become intoxicated by the fumes. I unfortunately am not a morning person. The rest of my family are. I'm wearing my plastering/painting clothes now for the last time in what I hope is a long time, and I'm pretty much done. I've managed not to drive myself crazy with all this ──D time alone to think, with the aid of what is now very well-known music to me. I have gained quite a bit of experience in caulking, artistically texturing, and painting, and above all, I can now be very proud of myself for a great accomplishment all my own . . . *"Let me sail, let me sail, let the Orinoco flow; let me reach, let me beach on the shores of Tripoli; let me sail, let me sail, let me crash upon your shore; let me reach, let me beach far beyond the Yellow Sea . . ."* ("Orinoco Flow"—Enya)	the excellent control exhib- ited overall. The student made use of a variety of language fea- tures, such as: J. Effective word choice to cre- ate sensory appeals; K. Parallelism, and; L. Interior mono- logue.

Figure 5.2. *(Continued)*

This stocktaking supports having students take responsibility for their own academic progress and fosters a problem-solving approach. The process causes students to determine why they are not performing and what assistance is needed. Many students need extra help, and stocktaking can bring this need to light. The discussion during the process is on the student's work and the standards rather than on more emotional issues such as attitude and work habits. The stance is always that all students are expected to work toward attainment of the performance standards, and that students should support each other.

Peer Review

To help students judge whether their work is good enough to go in the portfolio, the teacher, in addition to posting the rubrics, may have students respond to each other's efforts by writing commentaries. These commentaries cause students to consider the quality of student work in much the same way that New Standards (1997) does in choosing samples of student work for the standards books. In fact, learning to construct commentaries is almost essential in learning to judge student work. For example, to produce commentaries for the writing standards, students have to apply the rubric descriptors and exemplify them with specific chunks of writing.

If students are able to do this analysis, they should then be able to construct pieces of writing built around the rubric descriptors. Once familiar with the descriptors and understanding their importance relative to the quality of a piece of writing, students increasingly gain sophistication as writers by seeing these descriptors play out in a variety of ways. Writing the commentaries makes explicit the "felt sense" of what constitutes good writing.

Grading

Grading and reporting to parents early in the year are a separate issue from evaluating students' progress toward the standards. To determine grades, the teacher uses a number of measures, including grades on tests, essays, class work, and projects and a percentage of portfolio entries. For the essays, the projects, and some of the class work, the teacher uses New Standards (1997) rubrics and then translates the levels of the rubrics to numerical equivalents.

The portfolio work done during each reporting period is factored into the student's grade report with a clear understanding on the part of students relative to what percentage of the total grade the portfolio work constitutes. For example, a reading log with a specific number of entries, or a persuasive writing entry, could easily translate into 15 to 20% of an entire end-of-grading-period grade.

Summary

Teachers who have been working in a traditional classroom will need to make a number of changes in their own attitudes, thinking, and knowledge if they are going to make the shift to a standards-based classroom. Our English teacher had previously provided lessons that developed students' skills in producing narrative accounts, but was less familiar with teaching reflective essays. She needed to increase her own understanding of the various genres, and needed to become familiar with the related scoring criteria and to develop consistency in her scoring practices.

Fortunately, our teacher had a lot of support from other teachers in her department and in other departments. They all realized the necessity of increased planning and coordination. She also had a lot of support from principals, parents, and the district. It was a lot easier to implement a standards-based classroom when the work she was doing was reinforced at all levels.

Note

1. The student performance standards in New Standards (1997) are used throughout this chapter. The document includes standards in English language arts, mathematics, science, and applied learning. The National Center on Education and the Economy has developed workshop and school-based tools to help with the many key tasks described in this chapter.

6

Beyond the CIM
Pathways to the Future

Jacqueline Kraemer
John Porter
Marc S. Tucker

THE CERTIFICATE OF Initial Mastery (CIM) program would ensure that all students are helped to meet the same high standards for a solid academic foundation. But a strong CIM program is only the first step. No matter how good a CIM program is, a CIM will have real meaning for students only if it is a gateway to the future. It must lead to something that students know is valuable and that will inspire them to work hard. We think it should be the gateway to a range of high-quality pathways for further education and training that promise young people good careers and a good standard of living.

In Chapter 2, "How Did We Get Here, And Where Should We Be Going?" these post-CIM options are broadly defined. They include post-CIM academic studies and post-CIM technical and professional studies. The academic studies programs consist of high-level courses, such as Advanced Placement (AP) and International Baccalaureate (IB) courses, which prepare students to apply to competitive 4-year colleges and, perhaps, receive college credit so that they can enter college with advanced standing. The technical and professional studies programs lead to industry-recognized skill certificates and associ-

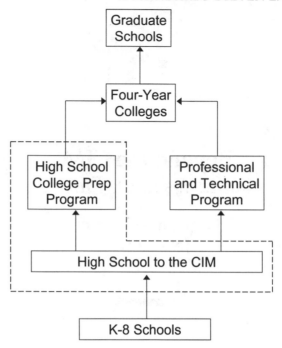

Figure 6.1. Post-CIM System

ate degrees (or credit toward those degrees) and qualify students for good entry-level career jobs in technical fields. The technical and professional programs also allow students to transfer credits into a 4-year college to complete a bachelor's degree if they wish.

Students are not "tracked" into one pathway or the other. The choice is theirs, based on their interests and career goals, and comes only after meeting the core standards represented by the CIM. In addition, both pathways are credible, real alternatives. Both offer rigorous academics, have explicit standards, and offer clear incentives for students. And both are pathways to 4-year colleges. There is no dead end (see Figure 6.1).

The proposal raises the issue of the future of the high school diploma. The certificate could become the diploma, or receiving the diploma could be made contingent on having received the CIM. Diplomas could be awarded in the future, as at present, on the basis of seat time to students who have disabilities so severe as to make it impossible to reach the standards and a small number of others who could do it but simply will not. There are good arguments for and against each option. We would let the states and districts make their own choices. Regardless, though, there are a number of feasible approaches to the adoption of the certificate idea and a high school diploma.

Let's look at how the post-CIM options might benefit two different types of students.

Roberto is graduating from high school this spring. He was fascinated by machines since he was young. He spent hours taking apart and putting back together the family appliances when he was a child. In elementary and middle school, Roberto excelled in school projects that involved building things. He struggled with reading and math, though, and often found school frustrating. By the time he was in high school, Roberto was enrolled in general-track academic classes as well as some vocational courses in the school's automobile repair program. He got by in his academic classes, but he preferred to be in the auto shop working on the cars there. Roberto assumed he would work in an auto shop after graduation, although he was not sure exactly how to go about looking for a job.

Roberto's cousin Julia has had an easier time in school. She loved school when she was in the elementary grades, and participated in a special enrichment program in grades 4 and 5. In middle school, it took little effort for her to get As and Bs, and she got her share, but she put most of her energy into extracurricular activities and the track team. Despite her good grades, she didn't find her courses very challenging. She could have learned a lot more, but no one ever gave her something she could sink her teeth into. High school was more of the same. By grade 12, she had fulfilled all her graduation requirements except for two classes and physical education. It was only when she was applying to colleges that Julia discovered that her As and Bs did not mean much. Her unimpressive scores on the SAT and the complete lack of AP or any other difficult courses in her record did not make her a good candidate for any of the selective colleges she had thought about attending. Looking back, Julia felt cheated by the system.

Many students like Roberto and Julia graduate every year—students with very little idea about how to get a good job or what kind of education and training they really need to prepare for one, and students who have done fine but have never been inspired to excel.

Students not heading directly to a 4-year college often "check out" of the academic process and coast through a mix of electives and general-track academic classes to complete their diploma requirements. Some enroll in vocational programs. Except in rare cases, though, these programs fail to provide the knowledge and skills needed to get entry-level jobs in careers ranging from auto mechanics to welding to computer programming to printing and graphics. Nor do they require the rigorous academics that are increasingly required for most good jobs of any kind. Students like Roberto are left to fend for themselves without the knowledge and skills they need for either the workplace or higher education.

Students like Julia also graduate, ostensibly having done fine. Julia is typical of a large number of students who are not thought of by their teachers as members of the academic elite in secondary school, but who have not been tracked into the vocational track either. She is part of the great mass of students in the middle, many of whom drift through school getting decent grades in courses without much academic substance and even less vocational substance. Julia will probably go to some kind of community or 4-year college, but she will almost certainly spend a lot of her time in college taking remedial courses. She is very likely to be among the majority of our college students, who take a full program for years on end but fail to get any kind of degree and, in the end, have little to show for her time in college. We have failed her, too.

How could a new kind of high school change things for Roberto and Julia? First, the focus on helping all students attain the CIM changes the logic of today's high schools by setting the expectation that all students meet the same high standards. There is no second-class curriculum for students like Roberto, and schools do their best to organize their programs and shape their instructional strategies to ensure that no one is left behind.

Through the post-CIM options, the program helps meet the unique needs and interests of each individual student. If Roberto had had an idea of what he needed to know to get a good job, he might have applied himself more in his academic classes. High school would have mattered. If Julia had had the opportunity to move on to more challenging classes in high school or a local college, she might have had something to which to aspire, a goal beyond fulfilling minimum requirements.

A New Academic Studies Pathway

Most people view the American system of higher education as the best in the world. But if college expenditures on remedial education are any measure, then we surely do have a problem. A large fraction of college entrants arrive with no more than an 8th-grade level of literacy and badly underprepared in many core subjects. Looked at that way, many 2-year college programs and not a few lower-division 4-year college programs are really high school programs.

The proposed CIM policy will end all that. High school students entering both 2- and 4-year colleges will be qualified to do college-level work. A much larger proportion of young people will be entering college. That will inevitably ratchet up college admissions requirements, and raise the level of all college education.

What might a post-CIM academic studies pathway look like? Every high school would have a coherent, challenging program designed to prepare students who have earned their CIM for college entrance examinations and to take college-level courses for which the colleges that accept them will give them credit. There are many models. The AP and IB programs are two examples that have the advantage of being nationally recognized and respected.

The AP and IB programs exemplify several characteristics that should be common to all post-CIM college prep programs. Compared to other tests used as entrance requirements in many colleges but not necessarily reflective of the school's curriculum, AP tests are linked to what students are learning, and AP courses are focused on helping students pass the examinations. Teachers and students know what to expect. Teachers use examples of test items in the course as a sort of practice test, and instructional materials are identified that will likely help students do well on the test.

On an international level, the 2-year IB diploma program offers another example of a coherent academic studies pathway. The program was designed as a comprehensive curriculum leading to a "baccalaureate" that can be administered in any country and is recognized by universities in every country. The courses of study are not only coherent, they are rigorous and emphasize a balance of learning in both humanities and sciences. Students are required to select subjects from each of six subject groups: first language, second language, individuals and societies (history, geography, economics, philosophy, psychology, etc.), sciences (biology, chemistry, applied chemistry, physics, environmental systems, and design technology), mathematics, and the arts and electives. They must take a mix of standard-level and higher-level courses to explore some subjects in depth and some more broadly.

The awarding of an IB diploma is based on a point system that requires students to meet defined standards within each subject. A variety of assessment methods is used to evaluate both the content and the process of academic achievement. Student work is judged by a worldwide network of examiners and is complemented by internal assessment of coursework by classroom teachers. Students must also complete requirements for an extended essay based on original research, a theory of knowledge course, and CAS (creativity, action, service) activities designed to educate the "whole person" and instill a commitment to community service.

The field is not restricted to the AP and IB. Some states have their own programs, such as New York State's Regents Program and California's Golden State Exams program. School systems could use these programs or develop and adapt other programs that contain similar characteristics and provide similar opportunities. An effective academic studies pathway should do the following:

- Provide challenging academic courses linked to assessments in a coherent system.
- Motivate students to excel.
- Support teachers in the delivery of the instructional program.

The benefits of each high school having a CIM program and a coherent post-CIM college prep program of this kind are incalculable. The need for remedial courses in college would be eliminated. Students would be much better prepared for college. They would get credit in large numbers for lower-division courses, saving them a great deal of time and money. All students would be qualified for college programs for which many now do not qualify. Students would be highly motivated to take tough courses and to work hard in school because colleges would be less willing to admit students lacking these qualifications. The frustration and disappointment of students who thought they were qualified for college and discovered later that they were not would be eliminated. High school staff, instead of trying to do everything and doing it badly, would have the satisfaction of doing one thing very well.

Many school people argue that the current college track in the high school suits our needs. In many cases that is true, but it is also true that the current high school system is frequently plagued with incoherence and inconsistency from classroom to classroom. The district, school, or department may have a syllabus, but there is no way of knowing whether teachers are using or have even seen that syllabus. Likewise, we don't know if students in a classroom are actually learning material or what their grade in the course really means; the same essay graded in the same school by two different teachers can be two letter grades apart, so what does a grade point average mean? It is very discouraging for students to think they are progressing successfully on a college-bound path and then later to discover that their performance does not meet college standards for admission, they will need to take remedial courses, or they are falling behind in college courses because they lack prerequisite knowledge.

It would help if high school assessments were aligned with college assessments used to determine admission and remedial courses, and if the high school curriculum were linked to those assessments. Such a system requires a high level of collaboration between high schools and colleges, but is in the best interest of both institutions.

Inevitably, policies of this sort will lead to agreements between the state postsecondary system and high schools like those in Oregon. In these, the state higher education system not only agrees to admit to nonselective institutions every student who has the CIM, it also makes it clear which high school courses and which grades get what kind of credit in the state higher education system. These articulation agreements greatly benefit both the high school and the state higher education institutions.

In all these ways, the academic studies pathway in the new American high school will do a much better job than the current system of preparing students for college-level work and ensuring a smooth transition between high school and college.

Student Motivation

Why would students be motivated to work as hard as they will have to work in these new post-CIM programs? Partly, the reward will be intrinsic, the satisfaction of learning a lot and mastering material that everyone knows to be difficult.

But for many, the rewards will be mainly extrinsic. Many colleges offer incentives to students who successfully complete advanced courses. With the AP program, for example, most colleges offer college credit against a general studies requirement for students who pass the AP exam (obtaining a score of 4 or 5) in a particular subject area. Thus, in many cases students are able to fulfill course requirements early.

Similarly, students who complete the IB program are eligible for admission to selective universities throughout the world, including Oxford, Cambridge, Harvard, Yale, Heidelberg, and the Sorbonne. The International Baccalaureate Organisation has formal agreements with many institutions, and some universities offer advanced standing or course credit to students with strong IB examination results.

Teacher Support

The kind of academic studies pathway described here requires a high level of professionalism and commitment from teachers and other staff. In fact, the pathway cannot succeed unless teachers deliver the program in a way that helps students succeed in passing the necessary assessments and making the transition to college. Therefore, the new academic studies pathway should include a strong teacher support component.

The IB program provides teacher training and information seminars, electronic networking, and other educational services to participating schools. In the AP program, there is a national network of teachers in a given subject area. Teachers have an opportunity to discuss curriculum materials, strategies for helping students do well on the AP exams, and related areas of interest. There is also an advisory panel of teachers who get together every year to review the exam. AP exams are scored by teams of teachers in the region based on rubrics and criteria for good student work. This system provides an excellent professional development opportunity for teachers by increasing their familiarity with the standards for student work, which helps them not only in scoring other students' tests but in designing their own classroom instruction.

When teachers are supported in these ways and are provided the kind of curriculum, assessments, tools, and student incentives described above, the possibilities are endless. Student mastery of a serious academic program can be a reality—not for just a few "gifted" students but for any student who has completed the CIM standards and wants to develop further proficiency in key subject areas.

A New Professional and Technical Studies Pathway

Until recently, the American economy was able to offer good jobs to workers with little in the way of academic knowledge or vocational skills. But things have changed. An increasingly competitive and technologically driven global economy has meant that industry needs workers who have strong academic and technical skills and can think creatively, solve problems, and work well with members of a team. It is becoming difficult to earn a good living without these skills.

Let us clarify two things before we continue. First, "skilling up" the workforce is not just about reforming the high school. The kind of advanced training that is increasingly necessary for good jobs is not something that can be provided through a series of introductory courses at a comprehensive high school. The faculty, equipment, relations with employers, and overall management required are too specialized and demanding. Regional technical and vocational high schools, community colleges with strong vocational, technical, and professional programs, and technical colleges (along with employers) will most likely need to be the providers of this kind of technical training.

The example of auto mechanics makes the point. For most Americans, the image of high school vocational education is closely identified with the image of high school students standing around cars in the auto shop in their shop clothes, holding wrenches in their hands. Most Americans may not know that in many states, the automobile dealers, which is where the good jobs for auto mechanics are, no longer recruit their new hires from high schools, but have worked with state higher education authorities to set up 2-year degree programs for auto mechanics in the state community college or technical college system. Teaching someone to repair a car can no longer be done by the watch-me-do-it-and-then-try-it-yourself method. The most important parts don't move. They are electronic and require abstract knowledge to diagnose and repair. High schools can no longer afford the equipment or the instructors needed to offer a first-rate auto-repair program, and dealers cannot afford to hire applicants who cannot function at a high level coming into the shop.

Second, it is worth a moment to consider how this new technical and professional studies pathway relates to the school-to-career transition-system-building initiatives going on across the country. It will be directly related to the school-to-career system if that system includes advanced technical training for young people. School-to-work has often been defined and operationalized without this piece, however. Most school-to-work initiatives have been limited thus far to career education and career-focused applied learning aimed at helping young people learn basic academic subjects and workplace readiness skills. Students in these programs may get a broad introduction to an occupational area or to the world of work, but not the advanced technical skills needed for good careers. This is not a criticism of current programs, just a recognition that another piece of the system needs to be built.

Elements of the New Technical Studies Programs

If vast numbers of young people are truly going to be able to prepare for and find good careers, a structured pathway to advanced technical skills is a vital, if sometimes missing, piece of the new system. The kind of technical studies programs we have in mind should:

- Consist of a program of rigorous technical studies and structured work-site training supervised by work-site mentors.
- Lead to industry-recognized skill certificates and associate's degrees (or credit toward such a degree) with articulation agreements that allow students to transfer to 4-year colleges.
- Require strong employer participation in program design, oversight, and student assessment as well as incentives such as job guarantees or preference in hiring for graduates, if possible.

Like the academic pathway, the technical and professional studies pathway must also:

- Provide challenging academic courses linked to assessments in a coherent system.

- Motivate students to excel.

- Support teachers in the delivery of the instructional program.

Many existing tech or prep programs, career academies, cooperative programs, and other career-oriented programs could be adapted to fit into the structure we are proposing, although few would meet all these criteria now.

A Program of Rigorous
Technical Studies and Work-Site Training

The best technical programs have always combined classroom instruction with practice. Programs in the new technical pathway should do the same. The curriculum would consist of applied academic courses, theory courses in the technical area, and practical instruction building on a student's experience in a work site. The applied academic courses would not repeat the academic core already mastered in the CIM program. These would be more advanced or specialized courses needed for the technical specialty. For example, a program in manufacturing might require statistics. Theory courses might include electronics or principles of hydraulics. Students also need to be given the option of completing whatever additional academic classes are required for an associate degree not required for the skill certificate.

The other key component of the program is work-site training. This on-the-job or apprenticeship approach is how most technical training around the world occurs and is part of many programs throughout the United States, including youth and adult apprenticeships, cooperative education, and many tech-prep programs. The work-site training can be arranged in different ways: a summer placement, a year-round placement, a full-time semester placement, or a placement on alternate weeks to allow for modules of full-time classroom instruction. A key to making the work-site component a success is to ensure that it is structured to correspond to what a student is learning in the classroom and the student is given a progressive and comprehensive introduction to the job and the industry.

Having mentors is one way to ensure that work-site training meets these objectives. Many apprenticeship programs in the United States have adopted the German concept of a workplace *meister,* or mentor, who coaches the student, assesses the program, and is the liaison to the educational institution where the student is attending classes. A work-site mentor can help a young person receive a structured introduction to the workplace.

Credentials With Meaning: Skill Certificates and Associate Degrees With Crosswalks to 4-Year Colleges

Credentials that have real meaning for technical programs are those recognized by employers which define the knowledge and skills needed for entry-level work in a good career job. These skill certificates should define standards for a broad range of jobs in which the work is similar, so as to give young people as much flexibility as possible to move around within an occupational area if they decide or need to change jobs. For example, a student could specialize in manufacturing for the aerospace industry and obtain a certificate in manufacturing. But if the aerospace industry undergoes a slump, the student could retrain in another manufacturing specialty (such as equipment repair) and not have to start over from scratch.

Unlike most other countries, America has no national system of technical credentials. We currently have a vast array of degrees and certificates that make it hard for either employers or students to make much sense of what is out there. In 1994, however, Congress created a National Skill Standards Board to work with business and industry to oversee the development of a system of voluntary occupational skill standards. The board is designing new broad-based standards to prepare young people in broad occupational areas, with many specialties within each area. Once these standards come on-line, industries and states can adopt or adapt them and training providers can develop programs that lead to them.

There also need to be articulation agreements with 2- and 4-year colleges to grant credits for the classroom work that is part of the technical program. This may be straightforward if it is already a program of a technical or community college, but other institutions will need to formalize agreements. This credit ensures the student an academic credential (or credit toward one) that allows him or her other options, and ensures that the academic work in the program is of college level. In some cases, additional courses may need to be taken to fulfill all the requirements for the associate degree (such as a foreign language or a writing class). In addition, work needs to be done to gain academic credits for workplace experience. Maine's Technical College System, for example, recently created a new associate degree in workplace proficiency that allows students to earn credit for work experience. But this is rare.

Crosswalks to 4-year colleges are a critical element as well. Agreements should be reached to allow a student to continue education in the technical area in which the student has specialized (such as a bachelor's in manufacturing technology), as well as in a broader range of subjects if he or she decides to change direction. Again, this may mean needing to structure opportunities for students to take additional courses to meet entry requirements for a bachelor's program. At a minimum, these pathways and the requirements to get there must be made very clear to students.

Driving the System:
Organizing Employer Participation

The role of employers in creating this type of pathway with programs of real value to students cannot be overemphasized. It cannot be accomplished without active involvement of employers. Employers are, in one sense, the ultimate customers of a technical training system. They need to define standards for these programs and ensure that the quality of those standards is upheld by participating in the assessment of students. They also need to offer work-site placements for students and work-site mentors.

Many communities have developed intermediary groups to organize this participation because it is sometimes difficult and too time-consuming for employers to organize partnerships with many different educational institutions, to offer work placements to many different students, and to be involved in the administration of a program. This is particularly true for small companies, which often cannot afford to assign someone to work on training activities. In some communities, companies have pooled funds and created their own nonprofit organization to work on workforce training initiatives. In other communities, an existing institution such as the chamber of commerce might perform this function.

These organizations often take on a range of functions, from matching students with workplace sites and work-site mentors, to processing stipends or paychecks for students, to offering training to mentors or organizing programs to let teachers intern in companies to get a taste of the workplace in which many of their students are spending time.

In addition to a role in management, employers need to communicate to young people that they value the credentials. Employers may be encouraged to announce that they will give preference in hiring to young people with CIMs and skill certificates. The idea that students have a piece of paper that certifies to prospective employers that they possess a specified set of knowledge and skills and can perform at a specified level is very attractive to employers.

Foundations of the New Technical and Professional Pathway

Although the crux of a new school-to-career transition system is rigorous technical training programs that lead to good jobs and further education opportunities, these programs must rest on a solid foundation of skills and information developed over all the years of schooling. In addition to the academic knowledge and skills that are the core of the CIM, this must include the following:

- Applied learning skills
- Career education that introduces young people to their post-CIM education, employment, and training options
- Career counseling systems that help young people make wise decisions about these options

Applied Learning Skills

Applied learning can be broadly defined as the capabilities people need to be productive members of society. Individuals need to be able to apply the knowledge gained in school and elsewhere to analyze problems and propose solutions, to communicate effectively and coordinate actions with others, and to use the tools of the information-age workplace. These are not basic job skills: They are skills all young people need for any kind of work or higher education. Applied learning skills are part of how we define a CIM.

Applied learning instructional strategies are particularly critical in preparing young people for their post-CIM options. First, applied learning strategies can engage students who are otherwise disengaged in learning. For example, a project requiring students to measure the pollution level of a local stream can help a student understand why science and math skills are important. Second, career-focused applied learning projects and programs can "hook" students early in understanding not only how academics can be applied, but how students personally can use academic learning to prepare for a real career after high school. Occupationally focused programs that teach core academics are a perfect example of this. Third, bringing a career focus into the curriculum broadly is a way to convey the career information young people need to make good decisions after high school.

Many states and school districts have begun to add language requiring workplace readiness skills, although few places have gone beyond vague statements of what is needed for success in the new labor markets. There are rarely performance requirements for these statements. One notable exception is the applied learning performance standards developed by New Standards (1997). New Standards identifies five applied learning standards, with performance standards for each:

- Problem solving
- Communication tools and techniques
- Information tools and techniques
- Learning and self-management tools and techniques
- Tools and techniques for working with others

Career Education

It is critical to provide all students with the information they need to make good decisions about their post-CIM education and training pathways. Career education should take different forms at different grade levels, progressively becoming a more intensive and time-consuming activity.

At the elementary level, students should be exposed to the world of work and begin to understand the different kinds of jobs available. Question-and-answer sessions with workers from the community, reports about a family member's profession, and similar assignments may be linked to the core academic standards of the school. By middle school, students should be involved in more intensive career education experiences, including job shadowing and internships at local organizations. By high school, career information activities should be more focused, allowing students to investigate and "try out" a particular area or specialty. By this point, many students might be part of a focus program where they are learning basic skills needed for a broad cluster of careers. Schools should also organize visits to some of the institutions young people might attend after high school to help them learn about the programs.

Finally, schools should also be aware of other resources in the community that offer information about careers, labor market conditions, and education and training providers. Systems of one-stop career centers are currently being built across the country to offer the public just such information.

Counseling for Career Development

Students need adults to help them shape plans for the future. The current counseling system is inadequate. First, there aren't enough counselors. Typical school counselors serve hundreds of students. And they are not just addressing postsecondary issues. Counselors are expected to deal with the gamut of personal and social concerns of students, leaving little time for serious career counseling. Second, most of the information counselors have about postsecondary options is about college. Counselors have little familiarity with the world of work, much less with what employers require. They are not usually trained to know these things. These factors result in very weak career counseling programs, which are often particularly detrimental to disadvantaged and minority students with few other resources for this advice. Clearly, we need to rethink how we provide career counseling to ensure that counselors have the time and the knowledge to do this critical job well.

Building the Technical and Professional Studies Pathway

There is no right way to go about building a post-CIM system of technical and professional studies for young people. Every school and every community must find its own way to organize these pathways.

Some communities will have existing tech-prep or youth apprenticeship programs that can be adapted to the new structure, whereas others will need to start from the ground up and build a consortium of institutions that together can provide the kind of training necessary. Some will choose to build pre-CIM focus programs that lead directly to advanced technical studies programs to create a seamless pathway for students. Other high schools will let the technical or community college system take the lead, and focus on helping students make good choices.

The task of organizing the technical studies pathway is made difficult by the lack of national occupational skill standards in most communities. With no set of skill standards around which to build programs, communities must improvise, develop, and adopt the best kinds of standards they can find that can meet the needs of employers to use in the interim. Communities can use the framework proposed by the National Skill Standards Board as a starting point for identifying or adapting standards.

But that doesn't mean we should or can afford to wait. Students such as Roberto need a different kind of education system and we owe it to him to work as hard as we can now to start building one. Below are two case studies of different communities that have begun to build the new technical studies pathway. The two cases are quite different. One is a program at a single high school in Chicago organized by a national industry association. The other is a statewide system of technical programs organized by the technical college system.

The Equipment and Technology Institute: An Industry Association-Driven Effort

The Associated Equipment Distributors Foundation (AEDF), the education arm of the construction equipment industry's association, represents companies that manufacture and distribute every kind of machine used in construction, material handling, logging, mining, and other related industries. The equipment industry's total sales and service are above $17 billion, and it includes such industry giants as Caterpillar, John Deere, Ford, Volvo, and Komatsu. AEDF represents 1,200 independent distributor and manufacturing firms.

Like many other industries in the United States, the equipment industry faces a shortage of qualified equipment technicians who can service the sophisticated machines used across the nation. The employment situation in the industry was becoming so dire that AEDF decided it needed to take bold steps to address the problem.

AEDF's first step was to define the broad skills and competencies the equipment and technology industry requires from its entry-level workers across all types of companies. AEDF used the framework proposed by the National Skill Standards Board for this work, with the hope that its standards could eventually be aligned or linked with those endorsed by the board. AEDF called its entry-level position "equipment service technician." It then identified five areas of knowledge and skill that a typical technician would need: diesel engines/ fuel systems, hydraulics, electrical/electronics, power trains, and safety/administration. For each, performance criteria to determine whether people met those skills were also identified. Finally, AEDF defined a career path for the equipment service technician from entry-level technician to journeyman to field technician to specialist/ master technician to foreman/supervisor, and the education and training needed to progress along this path. AEDF also detailed the kind of jobs in other related industries for which young people would qualify with each level of education and training so as to keep as many options open as possible.

Armed with a map of the skill needs and employment pathways, AEDF approached a community to design a program that could train young people to meet these competencies. AEDF, located in Chicago, decided to start work in its own backyard. The foundation put together a coalition of Gage Park High School and several postsecondary institutions to begin planning a new program. The group decided that it needed to begin working with students while they were still in high school. The notion was that it could introduce students to the field (of which it thought students were not aware), help them meet entry requirements for a postsecondary program, and then help them complete the postsecondary program.

The program AEDF designed, the Equipment and Technology Institute, is a 3- or 4-year school-within-a-school that combines high academic standards in math, science, and language with the technical knowledge necessary for work in the field (see Figure 6.2). It takes place at Gage Park High School, in area businesses, and in a local community college (Daley College), a private vocational college (Universal Technical Institute), and a 4-year polytechnical college (Illinois Institute of Technology). Graduates of the program are guaranteed a

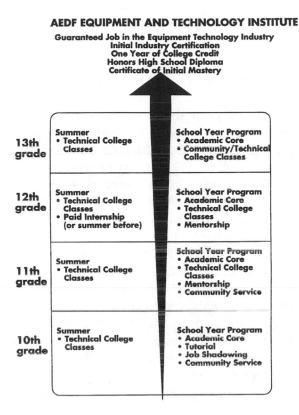

Figure 6.2. AEDF Equipment and Technology Institute, Gage Park High School, Chicago, IL

job in the equipment industry in the Chicago area. Students graduate with the following:

- Gage Park High School's honors diploma (which fulfills all college entrance requirements)
- A CIM endorsed by the Chicago public schools, AEDF, Daley College, Universal Technical Institute, and Illinois Institute of Technology
- A certificate from AEDF that recognizes the student as an entry-level equipment service technician with the basic skills to work for a member company anywhere across the country
- One year of college credit

AEDF has also negotiated articulation agreements with the involved postsecondary institutions so that students can take a few additional courses and receive an associate degree or transfer directly into a bachelor's degree program in manufacturing or a related technology.

Students apply to enter the program in grade 10. They sign a contract with the institute and with their parents or guardians agreeing to complete the program even if it involves an additional year of schooling. The program runs 12 months each year, including summer courses and Saturday and afternoon tutoring sessions.

After students have attained a CIM, they participate in a paid internship with an area company. Incoming students are assigned one Gage Park High School counselor for all 3 years of the program. The counselor is trained by AEDF to understand the needs and expectations of the equipment and technology industry—and the career opportunities within it. Students are assigned a mentor from the equipment and technology industry.

Business partners include companies that belong to AEDF, and they play a big role in the program. These business partners are expected to provide financial support (both directly for student stipends and salaries and indirectly through contributions to AEDF, which covers most administrative costs of the program); serve on the institute's advisory board; supply the program with up-to-date technical equipment; perform annual audits of different classrooms to ensure that what is taught pertains to the knowledge actually needed in the industry; supply students with business mentors, job-shadowing opportunities, a paid internship, and, ultimately, a job; participate in the program's speaker forum; and provide training about industry practices to technical and academic teachers as needed.

About 100 students entered the program in the 1997-98 school year. AEDF and Gage Park High School are now working to expand the program. The industry foundation is planning to replicate the institute at several other high schools, and Gage Park is adding another institute through a partnership with Daley College and the University of Illinois–Chicago. The program will eventually include 350 students.

Eventually, high schools should concentrate on academics and leave the technical and professional studies pathways to the community colleges, technical colleges, and other postsecondary institutions that can afford to hire specialized faculty and purchase the equipment needed for such programs, as well as maintain the web of employer relations needed to make the programs a success. But Gage Park shows what can be done by determined and creative people within the current framework of the American education system to create a "virtual" image of the system we have in mind.

Maine's Career Advantage Program

Maine's Career Advantage is a program of the Maine Technical College System in partnership with Maine high schools and businesses. The program was started in early 1992 as a pilot by the Maine Technical College system to offer students combined classroom experience and workplace training in one of several broad occupational areas. The governor at that time, John McKernan, had just returned from a trip to Europe with Maine Technical College President John Fitzsimmons where he saw programs that coherently combined classroom and workplace training. To bring this about in Maine, the two thought that a system of articulation between secondary and postsecondary schools driven by employers in the state should be instituted.

The program currently offers placement opportunities in a number of occupational areas and has organized a skill standards board to set the standards for a certificate of skill mastery in such areas as:

- Assembly technology
- Automotive management
- Banking and finance
- Biotechnology
- Civil engineering technology
- Computer technology
- Drafting technology
- Hospitality
- Electronics
- Manufacturing technology
- Metals
- Marketing and entrepreneurial management
- Public services
- Telecommunications

Students can begin the program the summer after their junior or senior year in high school. Both summer and career internships are available. Career interns continue the internships for two years with a company in the occupational area of their choice. They then continue the internship (or apprenticeship) for 2 years while they complete high school and attend 1 year of technical college. The students complete the program with a certificate of skill mastery in an occupational area and 1 year's worth of credit toward an associate degree in Workplace Technology. The students pay no tuition for the college courses and receive a stipend for their work. The participating businesses cover the stipend and tuition expenses.

Businesses must also provide a trained work supervisor, who is expected to act as both coach and mentor to the intern. Ideally, a supervisor should be able to communicate technical knowledge, provide emotional support and encouragement, and instruct the intern in how to succeed in the workplace environment.

The Maine Career Advantage organization functions as an intermediary for the partners in the program. Guided by a steering committee of leading state and international business leaders, organized labor, and educators, the organization offers training sessions for work supervisors and participating businesses and extensive orientation, employability skills training, social and community activities, site visits, and in-depth assessment procedures for interns.

Maine Career Advantage has expanded from its pilot site to all seven regions of the state served by Maine's technical colleges. In 1997, 3,950 students participated in the program, 300 businesses offered work placements, and 128 secondary schools and technical centers agreed to offer the program to their students.

Summary

The new American high school we have in mind is conceived in the ashes of the comprehensive high school, which it would replace. The comprehensive, something-for-everyone high school is a sorting machine. The new American high school is the opposite, an institution designed to bring all but the most handicapped students up to an internationally benchmarked certificate standard. As a practical matter, that standard is roughly equivalent to the requirements for college-level work in the majority of American colleges. It follows, then, that every student who gets the CIM is ready for college. Few, if any, high schools today can say that all but their most handicapped students leave their high school ready to take a college-level program without remediation.

Once the system is fully up and running, we would expect many, in some cases most, students to reach this standard by the time they have completed 10th grade. This leaves the question as to what they will do during the time now allotted to the upper division of high school. We proposed two options.

The first is to stay in high school for further academic studies. If students do that, they participate in a coherent college preparation program designed either to give them credit for introductory college courses or to prepare them for the examinations required by selective colleges for admission, or both. Such programs could include the IB program, a coherent program of AP courses, a state program (such as the Golden State Courses in California), or a combination of such courses.

The other choice a student might make when the new system is in place is to leave high school to participate in a program of professional and technical education, taken at a community college, a technical college, or a 4-year institution. These programs might vary in length for a full-time student from 3 years to 4 years, depending on the nature of the industry cluster the individual has selected. In most cases, these programs would include a mixture of classroom work, laboratory work, and on-site work in the industry. In all cases, the student would be working to get a skill certificate issued under the auspices of the National Skill Standards Board. These industry-developed certificates would be passports to good jobs, leading to good careers in a wide range of jobs typically covering several industries. Students receiving these certificates would also receive a 2-year college degree or credit toward one.

Whichever of these options the student picks after receiving the CIM, he or she ends up qualified to pursue a 4-year college degree. There are no dead ends in this system.

Programs such as the Motorola University program at Maricopa Community College in Arizona are shining examples of institutions that provide very high-quality professional and technical programs of the kind described here. The program in Maine is another. The program at Gage Park High School shows how a virtual institution that does the job well can be "assembled" from parts of existing ones. There are many others that are less well-known.

The low quality of technical and professional programs offered by many community colleges, technical colleges, regional vocational high schools, and other institutions has given them the reputation of dumping grounds. These institutions have often been starved of resources and relegated to the lowest rung on the status hierarchy of postsecondary education. That must change for our proposals to bear fruit. These institutions must have the kind of financial and social support that their counterparts in Europe and Asia have received. It is not too soon to begin.

Part III

The New
American High School:
A Standards-Driven System

7

A New High School Design Focused on Student Performance

Judy B. Codding
Marc S. Tucker

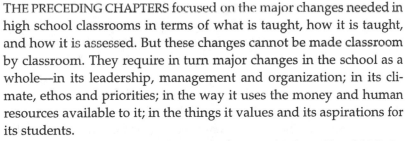

THE PRECEDING CHAPTERS focused on the major changes needed in high school classrooms in terms of what is taught, how it is taught, and how it is assessed. But these changes cannot be made classroom by classroom. They require in turn major changes in the school as a whole—in its leadership, management and organization; in its climate, ethos and priorities; in the way it uses the money and human resources available to it; in the things it values and its aspirations for its students.

In Chapter 2, "How Did We Get Here, and Where Should We Be Going," Marc Tucker presented the case for reassessing the place of the American high school in the whole scheme of American education. He made the case for conceiving of the overriding priority of high school as bringing virtually all students up to an internationally benchmarked level of accomplishment, ready to go on to a demanding four year college program without remediation or to embark on an equally demanding program of professional and technical education. This chapter accepts that goal as its premise, and acknowledges that the goal will require a thorough redesign of the high school.

That redesign will begin with the abandonment of the ideal of the "something-for-everyone" comprehensive high school and a recommitment to the ideal of academic excellence for all. Our analysis begins with a simple observation: Providing academic excellence for all is a full-time occupation for any high school. The something-for-everyone high school is a perfect match for the unfounded belief that only a few students can do serious academic work. The other students are left adrift with a bland general curriculum that contains math courses without math, science courses without any science, and so on. The vocational education of the comprehensive high school is equally insipid—an auto mechanics course that develops skills in fixing obsolete parts like carburetors and none at all in the repair of modern computer-controlled fuel injection systems. In almost every case, these high schools give as much weight to drivers' education as to physics, to a course in popular culture as to one in geometry.

Bringing every student up to an internationally benchmarked standard of academic accomplishment will require an unprecedented focus of resources on a much narrower curriculum. The so-called general curriculum, organized as it is around academic courses without any serious academic content, must simply be abandoned.

The vocational curriculum is another matter. There is a reason that most high school automotive programs are seriously out of date and most automobile dealers are now recruiting entry-level mechanics from the ranks of community college degree holders. The skill and knowledge levels required for almost every entry-level job leading to a good career have been steadily rising; it is now beyond the capacity of any high school to provide the range and depth of instruction in a wide range of technical subjects leading to such careers at the same time that it is trying to get every student up to a high level of academic accomplishment. The truth is that preparation for virtually all good careers—those that require four year college degrees and those that do not—requires a high level of academic accomplishment.

The modern high school must do one thing well—provide first class academics—rather than several things badly. Serious professional and vocational preparation should come after the student has the Certificate of Initial Mastery (CIM) and it should not be provided at the high school.

A high school that lets go of the general curriculum and of the vocational curriculum and commits to providing a high quality academic program for everyone, irrespective of their background or prior accomplishment, is a new kind of high school. That new kind of high school requires a new design. That design is the subject of this chapter.

Overview:
The Essential Elements of High School Redesign

We have argued that anyone who hopes to accomplish much at the high school level must, in some sense, take on the entire agenda at once. Here we lay out the bare bones of that agenda.

1. Provide a safe, clean environment for everyone
2. Decide on clear, high standards for student performance, focused on a coherent academic core that is the same for all students
3. Develop a sequential curriculum for the academic core, matched to the standards, with end-of-course assessments that assess what has been learned in each of those courses
4. Include in the curriculum strands for students who are working below grade level in the core, so there is a clear path for them to catch up
5. Create incentives for all students to take these new, tough courses and to work hard in them
6. Develop a school climate and organization that produces strong, personal support for each student and a feeling on the part of that student that the adults in the schools believe that the student can and will succeed
7. Create features of the school organization, management and governance structure that communicate to every member of the school community the expectation that every student is expected to reach high standards, as well as what each member of the community will be held accountable for with respect to that goal
8. Develop a school culture that focuses relentlessly on results and on getting every student to the standards
9. Provide strong support for every staff member to acquire the professional skill and knowledge needed to succeed in his or her job
10. Build community services and supports for the students outside of school, so that they are able to take full advantage of school

11. Help parents to support their children in school
12. Develop a school leadership style that is inclusive, making everyone, including staff, students, and parents, feel that they are welcome participants in the drive to improve results

In the rest of this chapter, we amplify each of these points in turn. Inevitably, as we do so, the educators reading this chapter are likely to say something like, "That all sounds fine, even right, but it is overwhelming. Where should I begin? How can I make it work in the real world that I face every day?"

To bring it all down to earth, as we go through these ideas one by one, we will tell you something about how Judy Codding dealt with these issues when she was principal of Pasadena High School. Codding became principal in 1988 and left 5 years later. PHS serves about 2,200 students, most of them African-American and Hispanic. A higher proportion of students in the school come from foster homes than in any other high school in California. When Codding took over as principal, the average score on the SATs was in the bottom quartile; 5 years later, when she left, the average score on the Math SAT was in the 57th percentile. That was not where she wanted it to be, but the gains that these young people made showed that they could learn much more than most of the faculty had ever believed.

Inevitably, Codding now wishes she had done some things differently. It is also true that she did some things to deal with problems you do not have, and that she did not have some problems that you do have. So we do not reflect on Pasadena in the spirit of providing a cookbook, but rather to illustrate some ways in which these things can be done in a practical way, as well as to stimulate the imagination.

1. Provide a Safe, Clean Environment for Everyone

You may be blessed with a high school in the suburbs that could not be cleaner or safer than it is. If so, skip right to the next section. Many high schools, however, are neither clean nor safe and, in some, both faculty and students come every morning in fear for both their lives and their property. In such places, it is almost impossible to improve the academic achievement of students until something is done to make the school a haven of order in what is often the chaos of the home and larger community. That is why this is the first item on the list. Where attention to this task is most needed, it is often the task that must be addressed first.

This was certainly the case at Pasadena when Codding arrived there. She discovered very quickly that many of the students roamed the campus, were consistently truant, were rude to each other and the adults, were involved in fights, had weapons in their possession and were getting in trouble with the law. Graffiti were everywhere around the 50 acres and 20 plus buildings on the high school campus. Codding knew that if the faculty did not address the behavior issues, they would never be able to improve student performance.

So she got the faculty and a group of student representatives together to develop a code of student behavior. She knew that the new code would never work unless the students had a strong role in shaping it because, in the end, it would have to be their pressure on their own peers that would change the behavior of the student body. Many forums were provided for discussion of what the new behavior code should be—the student government, homeroom, department meetings, faculty meetings, administrative meetings, and parent meetings. When these discussions were completed, the faculty, administrators and students drew up a short list of rules and consequences that would be uniformly, consistently and fairly enforced. These rules and consequences were professionally printed on 11 by 14 construction paper, posted in every room in the school, mailed out to all parents and discussed in parent meetings, and discussed in all classes, homerooms and grade level assemblies.

The gist was simple. Students with weapons would be removed from the school immediately and not permitted to return. There would be no graffiti on the grounds; students caught spray painting graffiti on the grounds would be required to remove the graffiti and their parents would have to come in for a session with the student and the principal before the student was permitted to return. Similar penalties applied to students who were caught fighting on campus, were roaming the campus and were constantly truant.

One of the most important keys to the success of these initiatives was involving the students and staff in the administration of justice under this system. Not only did the students and staff participate in devising the rules, but a student and staff panels (by house, to be discussed later) also recommended punishments for students caught infringing the rules. The punishments they recommended were often tougher than those the faculty came up with.

2. Decide on Clear, High Standards for Student Performance, Focused on a Coherent Academic Core That Is the Same for All Students

Our critique of the modern high school is that its agenda is diffuse, its expectations low and its standards unclear. It follows that we would have a high school with a highly focused agenda, high expectations for everyone and clear standards that reflect those expectations and make them concrete.

The first decision to make is what is the academic core. For us, that would include English; mathematics through algebra II, including algebra, geometry, probability and statistics; science, including physics, biology, chemistry and earth sciences; history, economics, and geography; music and art; and physical education. When we say "academic core," we are referring to a core of subjects that every student is expected to master to a predetermined standard, irrespective of what they will do when they leave high school. As you can see from the list we just shared, this conception of academic core would leave little time for electives, assuming that one is expected to master the core in order to get the CIM before going on to the upper division college-prep program, or getting their diploma and going on to a professional and technical education program. If some students are to get the CIM by the time they are 16 years old, and the rest before they finish high school, then all the courses needed to get the CIM would have to be available to be taken in sequence during the first 2 years of high school. Your state probably has its own standards in some or all of these subjects. It may or may not require a particular level of mastery of some or all of these subjects for a student to get a diploma. You will have to start with your state's minimum requirements and decide what you want to add. In any case, you will need to have a set of performance standards for completion of the CIM program, which is the same as saying that you will need a set of performance standards for the successful completion of the core curriculum. By performance standards, we mean standards that make it very clear what kind of student work meets the exit standard for each subject in the core.

When Pasadena took on this task, there was nothing in place at the state level to guide the school. California did have a well respected set of curriculum frameworks, which did not prove to be very useful because they provided no way for a teacher or student to know what quality of work to expect of students. The Pasadena school district had only minimum graduation requirements set forth in terms of Carnegie units a student had to accumulate and a bare-bones minimum competency test students had to pass to get their high school diploma. PHS had to start from scratch.

In 1988 the performance profile for Pasadena's students was dismal. The school had a real drop out rate of at least 36%. Of the students who stayed in school, close to 50% received Ds and Fs in English, math, science, and history. Approximately 30% of the entering ninth grade students were socially promoted from the middle schools and the freshmen class entered in the bottom quartile on the SATs.

PHS's students were failing across the board, and the school could not work on everything at once. Clearly English and math were the keys to all the other subjects. It was pointless to set history and science as priorities if the students did not have the basic skills in English and math to succeed in these subjects. English and math would have to become the focus of all the school's efforts.

But the faculty wanted a more specific target. Fortunately, the College Board had just come out with a report that showed a very high correlation between passing algebra and geometry in high school and later academic success. The faculty decided that this was a target worth shooting for. PHS would try to get Pasadena's students to a solid level of competence in reading, writing, algebra and geometry by the end of 10th grade. It would use the University of California tests of algebra and geometry as the standard for math and the SATs to set the standard for English. After that, in grades 11 and 12, the focus would be on history and science, but the faculty would, even then, continue to work very hard on the students' reading, writing and math skills and knowledge.

So the academic core at Pasadena consisted of reading, writing, math through algebra and geometry, and, for those who could master these subjects, history and chemistry as well.

That was Pasadena. It was operating in a far more difficult environment than most high schools do. Most students will come to high school better prepared than these students did and most high schools will be able to set higher targets for their students than Pasadena could, provided that, like Pasadena, they concentrate on a highly focused core curriculum.

Assume for the moment that you have decided on the academic core for your school and assume, too, that the students know that they have to master that core to get their Certificate of Initial Mastery. Some of those students will get their Certificate by the time they are 16. Others will take longer. Now assume that some of your students, once they have the CIM, will leave the high school to pursue a professional and technical certificate at some other institution. But many will not. Those who stay will do so because they want to stay in your high school to take a demanding post-CIM academic program. They want to participate in that program because they are interested in getting into the best selective four year college they can or because they want to go to college with as much credit for introductory college courses as possible, or both.

That means that your second job, after you have decided on the pre-CIM academic core, is to decide on what your post-CIM academic program will be. You might decide that it will be the International Baccalaureate, an internationally recognized program that, if successfully completed, will get a student into many competitive colleges all over the world. Or you might decide to offer a coherent program made up of Advanced Placement courses offered by the College Board. These programs are recognized by most American colleges and many of those colleges will give students credit for college level introductory courses if they get a sufficiently high score on the exams that go with these courses. Some states offer designated courses and exams that incorporate the requirements of their higher education system—the Golden State courses in California, for instance—which could also constitute a candidate program for the upper division of your high school. You could offer one of these programs or more than one, if you could afford it and there was sufficient demand for it. Clearly, the upper division program could also include genuine electives, but our vision of the American high school would, at both lower- and upper-division levels, greatly restrict the variety of courses now offered and substitute for this endless variety a rigor and focus now too often lacking.

3. Develop a Sequential Curriculum for the Academic Core, Matched to the Standards, With End-of-Course Assessments That Assess What Has Been Learned in Each of Those Courses

Deciding on the subjects to be included in the core curriculum at the lower-division level and agreeing on the performance standards for each subject are only the beginning of the curriculum task. Next, each subject needs to be divided into a sequence of courses that begins at the beginning of the freshman year and can be concluded by the most able students by the end of the sophomore year. Each course in the sequence then needs to have a course design developed for it that will be used by all the teachers teaching that course in the school. We do not mean by this a daily lesson plan, but we do mean enough structure to make sure that all students, in all classes taking that course, are exposed to more or less the same material and have, therefore, a comparable shot at meeting the relevant standards. This is, of course, a major departure from standard practice, which, at least in theory, makes it possible for every teacher to develop his or her own syllabus according to his or her own taste—except, of course, in the Advanced Placement courses, the most desirable assignments of all for a teacher, where the course outline is provided by the College Board and is very clear.

Then an end-of-course examination should be developed for each course in the sequence. The exams, of course, should be matched to the standards and to the courses, which in turn are matched to the standards. In this way, every student can be sure that, with enough effort spent on the course of study for that course, he or she will be able to pass the exam at the end. These end-of-course exams will look very much like the exams that any good teacher would give at the end of the course, with some long essay questions and some short answer questions. In science, there might be a lab component that stretches over several class periods. In math, there will be some short and some extended problems to do. In English, the student will be asked some questions based on the literature required in the course of study, but might also be asked to write a memo, do an analysis of a newspaper editorial, and paraphrase a technical manual. When the student has passed the end-of-course exams for the last courses in the sequence, then that student will be awarded the CIM the school offers.

At Pasadena High School, it proved very difficult to find a sequenced curriculum that would get their students to the standards set by the University of California algebra tests. Codding asked the math department to make a set of recommendations as to what was needed to ensure that at least 80% of PHS's students would hit the targets they had agreed on. After much discussion the high school math department and district math coordinator recommended a highly respected new math series. After reviewing the series, it became clear to Codding that the recommended series might be good for the students who had a solid background in middle school math, but PHS's students would be lost with such a curriculum, because they almost wholly lacked the prerequisite skill and knowledge.

Codding and the Pasadena district's director of high schools agreed that they needed a program that was specifically designed to meet the needs of the student population but would not "dummy down" the curriculum. They began talking with people all over the country and eventually decided on Gil Lopez's program, the Comprehensive Math and Science Program (CMSP), a field based, research and development program organized as a collaborative effort blending the resources of the private sector, higher education and the generous support of the National Science Foundation.

This program was uniquely matched to Pasadena's needs. Instead of assuming that students beginning the program had a solid middle school math background, it assumed that students beginning the program knew very little math at all—which was true for these youngsters.

CMSP mandated among other things that all students not performing at 80% or better on a pre-algebra readiness test administered by the University of California at Los Angeles be placed in a double period of math every day for 2 years. One class period would focus on math skills and concepts and the other period would focus on math applications. The two-period course over 2 years would take students through algebra I and geometry and prepare all students for algebra II in the 11th grade. PHS set as its goal to have 80% of its entering freshmen class achieve this performance standard by the end of the summer of the 10th grade. Student performance would be assessed using external assessments developed by CMSP, not local teacher-made tests. This is the practice followed by the Advanced Placement program.

PHS was not as successful in reading. The faculty could not find any national program for high school students who could not read with understanding. So they ended up developing their own program, which was very wearing and time consuming for the teachers. Again, a double period was set aside for reading and writing every day for freshmen students who had demonstrated very low reading and writing skills, about 75% of the class. The students came to high school having read very little and not having much expected of them in writing. The program design was based on the premise that the best way to improve both was to get the students to do a lot of both.

Looking back on that experience, Codding wishes that the New Standards performance standards requiring every student to read 25 books a year had been available to the school then, because it would have made their work much easier. That should have been the target. More broadly, Pasadena would have found its job much easier if California had clear performance standards for math and English with matching examinations, and if a well-sequenced course of study had been available to get their students to the standards, accompanied by external end-of-course exams.

But the high school would still have had to build a math curriculum on the premise that the students coming to it from middle school knew little or no math. That is the issue to which we turn next.

4. Include in the Curriculum Strands for Students Who Are Working Below Grade Level in the Core, So There Is a Clear Path for Them to Catch Up

The standards we have in mind are much higher than the implicit standards for which most high school students are now held accountable. It follows that many, perhaps most, of your entering freshmen will come to your high school with less, sometimes much less, knowledge and skill than is required by your curriculum. In more conventional language, they will come to you way below what you will have defined as grade level for the freshman year.

We just told you that the math curriculum eventually selected by the staff at Pasadena High School, Gil Lopez's Comprehensive Math and Science Program, contained a rare but essential feature addressed to this issue. It was specifically designed to get all students to the standard, no matter where they started. Sequences of exercises were included to give students who were way behind practice of the kind they needed to catch up. These exercises were not just problems in computation. Every one was couched in terms of applying that knowledge to a real-world problem. It turns out that this not only makes the material more interesting, but, much more important, it makes the material much easier to grasp.

In Pasadena, 8 years ago, Lopez's math curriculum was a life saver. It was actually designed by Lopez and his colleagues for use at the middle school level, but it met Pasadena's needs better than anything else available. CMSP is designed to provide underachieving math students with a highly structured experience that includes the following:

- A four-semester sequenced math curriculum where students take two different math classes per day, one focused on computational and conceptual understanding and the other on application, taught by two different teachers who utilize the topics taught in one course to complement and reinforce the topics in the other
- Use of Title I money to support an intensive tutoring program that is provided during the regular school day, after school and in a Saturday morning program
- A contract signed by the students' parents in which they agree to have their son or daughter attend the extra support classes, if necessary
- A grading system of A, B, and no credit
- A requirement that the school provide an extended school year program in CMSP math for those who did not pass with an 80% score or better
- A requirement that the school provide a half-time CMSP math coordinator, purchase and use all CMSP material and tests, and provide intensive summer training for all CMSP math teachers

You are not, of course, required to use the CMSP curriculum. And, besides, that curriculum will not cover the range of courses in your core. So you will need to find some way to construct a curriculum that does in all the subjects what this curriculum did in a more limited range for Pasadena. Our organization, the National Center on Education and the Economy, has set out to develop standards-based curriculum materials in a range of subject matter that include this feature, what we call an on-ramp feature. The phrase comes from the design of interstate highways. The idea is that the students who are on grade level are already on the interstate, and students who are below grade level need an on-ramp that will enable them to merge into the at-grade-level flow of traffic smoothly. Others will surely follow. If you do not find what you want, though, build your own. This task, building a curriculum to enable below-grade-level students, is crucial and it is new. Sadly, we never used to worry much about the students who were behind. We simply labeled them lower ability students, put them in their own track and that "solved" the problem.

5. Create Incentives for All Students to Take These New, Tough Courses and to Work Hard in Them

One would like to think that if the high school curriculum was sufficiently interesting, the students would work hard to master it. But there is no evidence for that proposition. There are many other things that interest young people at that age, and, as matters stand now, only a few see a direct connection between working hard in school and the achievement of goals that they really care about. If that does not change, their achievement will probably not change much, because no curriculum will make a difference if the students do not study it.

In Chapter 2, "How Did We Get Here, and Where Should We Be Going?", Tucker argues that widespread implementation of the CIM would change the incentives operating on students radically. If the students know they are very unlikely to get into college or get a job leading to a decent career without such a certificate, they would be much more likely to take tough courses and to work hard in school. We know that because students have told us that and because the experience in every country that has such standards bears out our conclusion.

Most important, in those schools in the United States that have tried a program of this kind, the result has been just what we predicted—student effort and therefore achievement improved, often dramatically.

Pasadena was an early effort of this kind, particularly in the design of Pasadena High's Graphic Arts Academy. Here's how it worked.

The idea was to find a way to motivate Pasadena's students by getting them involved in a program that would pay off for them in terms that they could easily understand—employment in jobs with a good career potential and the opportunity to go on for more education. But that pay off had to be real and highly visible, not just words from the principal in a motivational speech in the high school auditorium. PHS decided to organize such a program around the printing industry, mainly because the southern California printing industry was desperate for qualified entry level workers and knew that it would have to collaborate with California's high schools to get them.

So PHS partnered with the Printing Industry Association of Southern California and a large local print shop in Pasadena. In addition, Pasadena City College, California State University, Los Angeles and the County Regional Occupational Program also joined the collaborative. Six months of design produced a Graphic Arts Academy with the following key components:

- The Graphic Arts Academy is open to all students in grades 10 through 12, including special needs students. All students are expected to meet the high academic standards developed by the partnership. Some students may take longer to complete the program than others

- Students are expected to learn both at school, either the high school or the community college, and at the workplace, a print shop

- The first year in the Academy is devoted to getting all students to high standards in reading, writing and math

- The core academic program of English, history, math and science is tied to the applied learning program in graphic arts. Teachers work together as a team and share total responsibility for the learning of their students

- The printing industry, higher education and the high school jointly set the standards and agree upon the curriculum

- Teachers and students have control over large blocks of time in their schedule

- All students in the program are assigned a business mentor to meet with them on a regular basis

- All students are required to take technical courses at the community college. Those students who successfully complete the coursework at the community college will have completed one year toward their community college associate degree while still in high school

- All students are involved in a paid apprenticeship program
- All students who receive the industry skills certificate are guaranteed a job by the printing industry when they complete the program

What's important here? First, the students who participated in this program understood from the beginning that at the end of the rainbow were: (1) a high school diploma, (2) a year of college credit, (3) an industry certificate stating plainly that they were qualified for jobs that pay well in the industry, and (4) a good job. Second, they understood that, in order to reach that pot of gold, they would have to meet high academic standards, and furthermore, the people who were running the program fully expected them to meet those standards.

Bear in mind that we are not advocating the use of the academy model in the new American high school. In fact, one of the things that Codding learned from the experience was how hard it is for a high school to get the attention from employers and assemble the technical resources required to mount such a program at a high enough level of quality. That experience at Pasadena is one of the reasons that we now believe that serious vocational instruction should not be part of the high school agenda, but rather the responsibility of institutions dedicated to that role.

What is relevant to the agenda we have described here is the way Pasadena used standards and the achievement of those standards to motivate the students in the graphic arts academy program. When the CIM we described above is endorsed by local employers and higher education institutions in the same way that this program was endorsed, the effects on the students are likely to be very much the same.

6. Develop a School Climate and Organization That Produces Strong, Personal Support for Each Student and a Feeling on the Part of That Student That the Adults in the School Believe That the Student Can and Will Succeed

So far, we have concentrated on showing how standards, courses of study, end of course exams, on-ramps and the CIM can be sewn together into a design for a high school instructional program that will get all high school students to high standards, providing them with a very strong academic foundation for anything they might wish to do with the rest of their lives. It is all standards based, at every level and in every way.

But the reader will recall that we did not start with standards. We started with personal safety and order, because, we said, safety and order are the necessary, if not sufficient, prerequisites for any program for raising achievement.

Safety and order, though, are only half of the coin, the tough half. The other side, personal support for each student, is no less important. It has often been remarked that the modern comprehensive high school could not have been better designed to produce anonymous, alienated students, students who feel no support coming from the institution or the adults in it, who experience high school as a place full of adults to whom students are at best invisible, adults who could care less whether students succeed or fail in school or later on in life. Because adolescence is most especially a time when we measure ourselves against the expectations of the world, hoping to find our place in that world, yearning to be part of something, to belong, the anonymity of our high schools is a singular disaster for untold thousands, perhaps millions of young people every year.

What Pasadena did about that was to divide the school into five learning units or clusters, which were called *houses*. One of the five houses became the international house, a transitional program for the bilingual students. Each house had its own teaching faculty and approximately four hundred students. In the ninth grade 50 students worked with three teachers—one who focused on reading and writing and two who focused on math in a three-and-one-half-hour block of time. In the upper grade levels four teachers made up a teaching team and worked with approximately 120 students in the same three-and-a-half-hour block of time. All students took a small number of elective classes such as physical education outside the house program. Each of the five houses had a head teacher, guidance counselor and support staff. All teachers in a house had common planning time built into the master schedule to discuss student progress, work on curriculum, problem solve around house issues, and meet with parents and guardians. All teachers were also members of their subject matter departments that spread across all houses. All professional members of the house served as an advisor to a group of students.

PHS changed its organization so that the teachers could really get to know the students and their parents and the students could start to believe that their teachers and the school cared about them as people and learners and would help them succeed no matter what. Prior to these changes, the 2,200 students had six different teachers with no two teachers having the same group of students so it was impossible for teachers to get together to discuss how to support individual students. Changing the way PHS was organized and managed helped make the school a place where the students felt they belonged and where they wanted to be. Giving each house faculty group its own block of time to meet with their students gave the teachers the flexibility to design their house master schedule in a way that best met the needs of the students in their house.

7. Create Features of the School Organization, Management, and Governance Structure That Communicate to Every Member of the School Community the Expectation That Every Student Is Expected to Reach High Standards, as Well as What Each Member of the Community Will Be Held Accountable for With Respect to That Goal

Every organization is a social system, and every social system has a way of communicating to its members what it really values What it values, of course, is not what it says it values, but what it shows it values by things that it rewards. It is very unlikely that faculty members will pull out all the stops to do everything that can be done to improve student performance when the school is constantly demonstrating that what it really values is something else, like loyalty to the principal, or keeping the people in central office happy, or keeping trouble down to a minimum.

One way to change the signals about what is valued is to change what the system formally rewards. A growing number of states and districts are doing this by setting minimum average scores for a school's performance and then putting schools whose performance falls below that point on academic probation. Schools on academic probation get a probation manager who must approve the school's budget and program plans and who has the power to recommend expedited dismissal of any professional staff member of the school.

These schools must also choose an external provider of technical assistance from an approved list. If such a school does not reach the minimum level of performance within a prescribed time, it is often dissolved. Some of these same states and districts are also setting up systems of rewards for schools that are able to produce better student performance each year than the year before.

One high school cannot, of course, set up such systems for itself. But a single school can act on the underlying principles involved. In the end, formal incentives of the kind just described are probably less important than the climate created by the principal. Which faculty members get praised for what kinds of actions? Who gets the plum assignments and who gets the dregs? Who gets to go on the special professional development trip and who does not? Who gets extra resources and who does not? The answers to these questions tell you everything about what the principal really values. When the answer to all these questions is, "The teachers who contribute most to improved student performance," then the school is poised to make real improvement in student performance.

At Pasadena, everyone quickly learned that whatever interfered with students acquiring the knowledge and skills they would need to achieve would have to stop. The most poignant—and difficult—example was the conflict that emerged between doing what was needed to get the students to the standards the school had chosen and the claims of the interscholastic sports program on the school schedule.

The CMSP program, as the reader now knows, required double periods of math and English. That time had to be found in the master schedule. But long California tradition provided that, during the last period of the day, interscholastic sports had primacy. The English or math teacher who was also a coach started the sports team practice during the last period, so that period was effectively unavailable for math and English, both for the teacher/coach and for the students on a sports team. Because of the complexities involved in scheduling both the students and the teachers, it proved impossible under these conditions to find the double periods the CMSP program called for in the master schedule. The demands of academics and sports had to be resolved.

In high schools all over the country, this would have been a no-brainer. Sports would have won, and the academic program would have had to make do. That is not what happened at Pasadena and the result was a "walk-out" by some of the teachers and students. But the principal and other administrators stuck to their guns. A compromise was reached that did not compromise the requirements of the academic schedule at all. In the process, an unmistakable signal was sent to every member of that school community that academic achievement was in fact, not just in words, the top priority of that school.

In Pasadena, the issue happened to be sports. For you, it will be something else. What is important is what you do when you are put to the test. What is important is not what you say, but what you do.

PHS was definitely a school that should have been placed on academic probation, had there been such a system. Had the school been on academic probation it probably would have moved at a much faster pace to improve student performance than it did. The school did have an excellent coach in David Marsh but he did not have the authority that a probation manager in, say, Chicago, has to make sure that the school is squarely focused on student achievement, nor were the consequences for faculty failure to improve student performance in place that are now in place in Chicago and a few other cities. All of those things would have made a big difference.

8. Develop a School Culture That Focuses Relentlessly on Results and on Getting Every Student to the Standards

The Taoists have a saying to the effect that water will always find its own level. This was the attitude we have generally had about high school students—the job of the high school—to provide an education suited to the students' abilities and interests. Our message could not be more different: All students must be educated to a high level, irrespective of ability and interest. Reaching that goal requires the undivided attention of every member of the faculty and an unrelenting focus on results.

Our colleagues at the National Center on Education and the Economy have developed a planning tool for this purpose, a tool we call Planning for Results. The spine of that tool is a series of questions that go something like this: What is our goal? How can our goal be expressed in terms of standards for student performance? How will we measure student progress toward those standards? Where can we find the most successful strategies that people anywhere have used to get students like ours to standards like these? How should we adapt these strategies to our circumstances? Who on our staff is going to be responsible for implementing these strategies? What is the deadline for implementation? Did we actually implement the strategy we chose? What does analysis of the data reveal about the degree to which the strategy resulted in student progress against the standards? What does that data suggest about the ways in which we need to modify the strategy to get better results?

Most school planning is done to comply with demands of people outside the school, and, for that reason, most school plans are shelved as soon as they are drafted. But a school that is seriously committed to results will plan carefully, and when it does so, is likely to find that it cannot achieve its objectives unless it makes major changes in well established ways of doing business.

The Pasadena story illustrates all these points. First, the decision to concentrate on reading, writing, algebra and geometry was made after careful collection and analysis of the data on student performance. The middle schools had given many of their graduates University of California credit for algebra I. So the Pasadena staff enrolled them in algebra II, which the students proceeded to fail miserably. So the principal administered the University of California algebra test independently to the graduating middle schools students, over the protests of the middle school principals. The students failed these tests badly. Now Pasadena High finally had the sound data they needed to plan effectively. That was what led to the national search for the right math curriculum to fit their students. It was the data that enabled the principal to say to the faculty that the highly acclaimed math curriculum they were proposing to use simply did not fit the students they were taking in from the middle schools. It was the constant flow of data that came from the independent CMSP tests that enabled the staff to figure out on a continuous basis what their students were having trouble with and what they needed to overcome that trouble.

Pasadena used that data as the engine of a planning approach that was a primitive version of the National Center's Planning for Results system, and it worked well enough to produce major gains in student performance over the 5 years. The data and the planning weighed heavily when the setting of priorities became contentious. When the confrontation over the priority given to sports in the last period heated up, the principal had the data on student performance and a sound plan for doing something about it which unambiguously required that the last period be devoted to academics.

The mother's milk of this kind of commitment to results is the constant flow of accurate data on student performance, not just at the end of the year, but all the way through the year—data that are gathered and analyzed for individual students, for a class, for a subject, for a subject at a grade level, for a subject at all grade levels, against other student data that might contain information revealing causes of low-performance, such as socio-economic data, data on national or ethnic background and so on. Do this well and you will find out that, for some students, the root cause of their math problem is a reading problem, for others the root cause of the reading problem is an eyesight problem, for others the cause is faulty mastery of the phonemic structure of the language, for others the problem comes from a mismatch between the culture of the school and the culture they are being brought up in, and for others, their mastery of the facts is fine but they are having real trouble mastering the concepts on which real understanding depends.

The image we are trying to convey here, then, is an image of a school committed to results, that uses a powerful planning system as the way to organize the efforts of the whole faculty to get those results, and is organized to provide the constant flow of accurate data on student performance on which the planning system depends for its effectiveness.

9. Provide Strong Support for Every Staff Member to Acquire the Professional Skill and Knowledge Needed to Succeed in His or Her Job

Creating an environment in which the high school staff is really focused on student achievement and implementing a planning system that serves to organize the faculty as it analyzes student performance and tries to do better are very important, but will not by themselves lead to improvement if the faculty does not have the skill or knowledge needed to do a better job than they have been doing.

Most professional development in public education consists of workshops that people in the central office think the teachers would profit from, on the one hand, and courses taken in education schools that are needed to get a degree.

Our view of what professional development should be is quite different. Lawyers, doctors, and other professionals assume that a very important part of their job every day and in every way is to keep up with new developments in their field that could affect their practice. And they are constantly seeking better ways to solve the problems that their clients present them with by finding out how other people in their profession are addressing those problems in the most efficient, effective way.

High schools should be organizing themselves to support this conception of professional development as an integral part of their strategy for getting all of their students to standards. There are two crucial questions here. The first is: How do we find out what we need to know to improve the performance of our students and how do we acquire the skills to do what we have to do? The second, which arises when the data reveal a particular problem with student performance, is: Who has done the best job of addressing this problem and how should we adapt their solution to our circumstances so we will get even better results than they got? This conception of professional development is very rooted in the particular situation, plans, and strategies of individual faculties. Professional development is what they do to get the skills and acquire the information they need to make their plan and carry it out.

This search for the best way to get the job done was a key element in the Pasadena strategy to achieve its math goals. One of the key strategies Pasadena used to provide the teachers with the knowledge and skills they needed to succeed with the students was an intensive summer training program for all teachers teaching in CMSP, combined with a monthly seminar for all CMSP teachers during the year. In addition all core teachers in the house program participated each year in an intensive summer professional development program during the first two weeks in August that was designed by the head teachers of each house and an administrative and teacher steering committee. This became known as Camp Codding. All these components of the professional development program focused on just one goal, the acquisition of the skills and knowledge the faculty needed to design and implement the Pasadena High School core program for student academic success.

But it was not enough to stay home. It was very important for the faculty to see other schools that were succeeding with students similar to those attending PHS, as well as to observe high achieving schools in general. Research reports alone do not provide a faculty the opportunity to find out what the people involved had to do to accommodate particular people or policies that your faculty does not have to accommodate, what they would do differently now, what their values are and how close those values are to those of your faculty, to get a "feel" for whether the program or strategy looks in practice the way it does on paper, or, most importantly, how the people who actually did it respond to your own ideas about what might work or the ways in which what they did could be updated or improved upon. For this, you have to go there.

So a team of parents, teachers, students and administrators went to New York City to spend several days at Central Park East Secondary School, visited other successful schools in the city and went to Greenwich High School in Connecticut to see their successful house program. After each visit the delegation spent considerable time discussing what it might take from the experience to improve student learning and opportunity at PHS. One summer, a group of teachers spent 3 weeks in an intensive professional development program offered by the faculty of Central Park East focused on student portfolios and exhibitions. The school also brought in people from other successful schools from around the country. For example, the person who headed the long standing advisory program at New Trier High School in Illinois spent time with the staff and students at PHS helping to design the PHS advisory program. What the school did is determine who in the country was doing a particular thing the best and either went to observe what they were doing or invited them to spend time at the school. The school did not believe that they had to invent everything themselves. They could use what others were doing, adapt it and even improve upon it for their own students.

10. Build Community Services and Supports for the Students Outside of School, So That They Are Able to Take Full Advantage of School

In some ways, young people are at their most vulnerable when they are in high school. Their parents typically do not supervise them very closely, partly because they know that they have to loosen the reins if their sons and daughters are going to mature the way they should, and partly because the tools for effective supervision are very weak by the time their children get to high school. The lack of parental supervision, combined with the anonymity of the typical

high school we described above, leaves many youngsters almost exclusively in the company of their peers. Even at work, the typical
Baskin–Robbins or McDonald's is an environment in which their
peers, not adult men and women, set the tone. For many suburban
youngsters, the peer group is dominated by young people exploring
the limits of drinking, drugs, and other forms of antisocial behavior.
For many urban youngsters, the peer group is the gang. For the
youngsters most at risk of dropping out, the environment outside of
school is all too often characterized by homelessness, parents who
cannot cope, no parents at all, a life of violence and drugs, or a grind-
ing poverty that undermines every effort to make it at school.

Rare is the high school where none of these problems is present.
Even those high schools that find themselves in relatively advantaged
settings have more of these problems than the casual observer would
guess, and far too many have the full range of problems we just
described.

Pasadena fell into the last category. The school formed a task force
focused on community services and supports where they struggled
to combine all the resources of the community into a one stop shop
for the students and their families. The school was only moderately
successful. They discovered that it is nearly impossible to do this
school by school. There needs to be a community resource governance
system put in place for all support agencies to work together. What
the school did do is bring together the probation services, provide
personal counseling, specific health care services, and job placement
and college counseling support. Everyone at the school would agree
that there needed to be a system developed to provide the comprehensive services that the students and their families needed. The
students and their families needed much more than the school was
able to provide.

Kentucky's comprehensive reform legislation created fully
staffed family resource centers for schools serving low-income students that serve as a place where faculty, parents and students can
access a wide range of health and social service agencies. When
students at the school are absent, the staff will find them and bring
them back to the school. When the school needs to talk to the parents
about a student, the staff of the center will facilitate that when necessary. Health and social services are available on the spot. Faculty
members at schools we have worked with in Kentucky constantly talk

about the difference these services make for both the faculty and the students.

11. Help Parents to Support
Their Children in School

We pointed out in the last section that parents' reins on their children are typically loosened by the time they start high school. The school is usually farther away from home than the elementary and middle schools their children attend. Their children have more teachers and take more subjects. And their children, no longer dependent in the same way that they were, are no longer so eager to have their parents around the school and talking with their teachers anyway. The high school faculty, more often than not, would just as soon not have to deal with the parents, because their experience of parents is either of angry people who are demanding that the grades of their children be raised, on the one hand, or the parents of misbehaving children who glower at their children and can't wait to beat them when they get home.

But the fact is that the participation of parents is just as vital in the high school years as it is earlier. Children of parents who do not believe they can achieve at high levels will not get the support they need at home if they are to achieve. Parental aspirations for and support of their children are often a decisive factor in a student's commitment to put in the time and the energy required to succeed. Most important, many, perhaps most, parents of high school age children just don't know what they can do to help their children succeed.

PHS realized right from the beginning of its restructuring effort in 1988 that parents and guardians would be one of the most important factors in improving student performance. Parents were alienated from the school. They never knew who at the school to call to find out about the progress of their children. When they got up the nerve to come, they would walk into the school and feel unwelcome. They as well as their children found the campus too large and impersonal. In some sense many parents had just given up. This could not have been more evident than in the Back to School night that Codding attended in October of her first year as principal when only about 200 parents showed up with a student body of over 2,200.

After that night parent involvement became one of three main goals of the school. But not the kind of parent involvement you often hear about, parents serving on school councils and other governing boards. The school had that but did not feel that would ever get the real engagement of parents that was necessary. With the redesign of the school into a house system, every student had a teacher advisor, and every house had its own full time counselor and head teacher. Every parent and guardian was informed of the name of the student's advisor, house counselor and head teacher. The advisors called the parents to introduce themselves at the beginning of the year. The advisors met with the parents and guardians twice a year. When necessary the entire teaching team (which included the student's advisor, head teacher, and counselor) met with the parents and guardians. The line of communication became clear to parents. If there was a question or problem in a particular course, call the teacher. If the issue is not resolved, discuss with the advisor, then the house counselor, head teacher, school dean, school assistant principal and then the principal. If the question or problem was not related to a particular class, the parent was asked to first start with the advisor and then follow the communication channel.

Of course this did not always work. Some issues were of such a serious nature that the parent or guardian started first with the principal. But the important point is that the parents knew their children had an advisor, an advocate, and could always find a voice who knew their child on the other end of the phone or across the table. By the second Back to School night, thanks to the hard work of the teachers and parent council, the school had over 2,000 parents and guardians present. Parents were indeed becoming partners with the school on behalf of their children.

12. Develop a School Leadership Style That Is Inclusive, Making Everyone, Including Staff, Students, and Parents, Feel That They Are Welcome Participants in the Drive to Improve Results

The movies and the folklore are full of stories of brilliant, dedicated principals who, single-handed, turned their high schools around. It is true that few schools are turned around without strong, effective leadership. But it is also true that no principal has turned a high school around alone. Leadership consists in identifying a goal that others feel is worth striving for and then inspiring and supporting everyone involved so they devote their full energy and commitment to reaching that goal. Mobilizing others is the essence of leadership; involving them in deciding what is to be done and how it will be done, so they make your cause their own is the only strategy that will work.

This is very hard work. Teachers everywhere have been treated more like blue-collar workers than professionals. They will say that they do not want to run the school, that they are content to do their own thing in their classrooms, that decisions about how money is spent is not something they want to stay after school to decide. As long as this is true, they have not taken and will not take responsibility for the achievement of the students in the school, for the way the whole organization works to support the youngsters who attend it.

So a strong principal is always tempted to make the decisions, and a weak one is typically eager to give them to the school-site council, which typically takes no responsibility for the results of its decisions. But the best principal will form a kind of cabinet of department heads and other faculty members, involve that cabinet in all the decisions that affect the life of that school, expect the cabinet members to reach out to the rest of the faculty in their respective areas, and hold the cabinet members accountable for the implementation of the plans that they develop.

There will be no results worth having unless (1) the principal takes the moral leadership required to make high student achievement the unquestioned first priority of the school, (2) people throughout the school's leadership structure feel directly accountable for producing that achievement, and (3) the people who will be held accountable have a direct voice in the decisions that affect them.

At Pasadena, these principles were acted on in many ways. First, as you have seen, most notably in the case of the conflict between the academic needs of the students and the demands of interscholastic sports as that conflict played out in the master schedule, the principal made student academic achievement the number one priority every time. These actions spoke louder than any speech on the subject and gave many faculty who had always shared these values the confidence that they could act on their convictions without being cut off at the knees by the administration.

Second, because it is important to make sure that decisions are made as close as possible to the people who will be affected by them, the principal gave many faculty members direct responsibility for many arenas of action that had a direct bearing on student achievement. Each department chair was responsible for overseeing the development of a well thought out, clearly sequenced program, building their department's budget, assigning teachers to classes and overseeing department policy. Each house head was responsible for overseeing the work and progress of all students and teachers in each house, building the house budget and coordinating the work of the house with the administrator assigned to their house. And many important issues that were school wide were treated in much the same manner. The reader will recall that when the school decided to address in a serious way the issue of community services and supports, the principal created a task force of faculty members and others to address it.

But these various assignments were not pursued without regard to the way they related to the school as a whole. The people who would be held accountable for addressing them successfully sat on the principal's cabinet, where they could present their views and proposals and have them considered in relation to all the other views and proposals before the group.

There was never any question in this arrangement that the superintendent would hold the principal accountable for the success of the students at Pasadena High School, nor was there any question that the principal would hold all those to whom authority had been delegated accountable for their part in producing student success. But, every person who was accountable had commensurate authority, and everyone who was affected by the decisions that were made had a voice in those decisions.

The sad truth is that we mainly "keep school," showing up every day to do "our best," accepting in the process a familiar web of constraints. Many of those constraints have to do with the needs not of the students but of us adults—the need of the community for school teams and players they can be proud of, the need of the central office staff to get their jobs done efficiently, the need of principals and other administrators to reward those who have been loyal to them, the need of the faculty to reduce the claim the school makes on their time outside of the regular school day, or the need of parents to get good grades for their students (deserved or undeserved). None of these motivations are illegal and none are immoral.

But our premise throughout has been that the touchstone of every decision that is made should be the degree to which it will advance not the interests of the adults but the academic performance of the students. More precisely, that it is premised on a commitment to making sure that all but the most severely handicapped will meet an internationally benchmarked standard of academic accomplishment.

That is an utterly different—and far more difficult—goal than the one pursued now by American high schools and there can be no question that it will require an utterly different design. Because we believe that the idea of the CIM captures precisely the core of the goal we have in mind, we have built a design around the CIM. We have laid a plan in which the conception of standards, assessment, curriculum, instruction, leadership, management, organization, planning, budgeting, accountability, incentives, professional development, the school's master schedule, and the involvement of parents, students, and faculty in all of these myriad activities revolves around the answer to one question: How do we get our students to the CIM standard and how do we help them build on it when they have reached it?

We will cling tenaciously to our goal, because we believe that it is right. But the design is only a means to that end. We invite you to consider it, try it and improve upon it. When you do, tell us what you did. If we all do that, we will all leave our high schools better than we found them. Which is all anyone can ask.

8

District Redesign
Direction, Support, and Accountability for Standards-Based High Schools

David D. Marsh
Michael Strembitsky

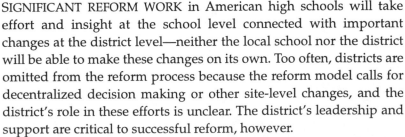

SIGNIFICANT REFORM WORK in American high schools will take effort and insight at the school level connected with important changes at the district level—neither the local school nor the district will be able to make these changes on its own. Too often, districts are omitted from the reform process because the reform model calls for decentralized decision making or other site-level changes, and the district's role in these efforts is unclear. The district's leadership and support are critical to successful reform, however.

Historically, high schools have had difficulty focusing on student performance, and the district office has often been part of the problem. For many high school leaders, the district office provides seemingly endless requests for reports, forms, data, and assistance. Unfortunately, the message from the district office, the school board, and the community is often that rules are crucial and risks are costly. These requests and these messages hinder the initiative of local leaders and push them to focus on merely getting kids to class, providing services and curriculum coverage, and avoiding "mistakes." This, coupled with a lack of real authority over the school program, has made school leaders settle for school survival rather than student success.

What should be the role of the school district in standards-driven secondary school reform? It will be quite a new role for several important reasons. The world is dynamically different now, with massive changes and an increasing pace of ongoing change. Fullan (1993) characterizes these as the new "change forces" that are dramatically influencing educational organizations (see also Hargreaves, Earl, & Ryan, 1996). But school districts have been slow to respond and lead in this new environment. For example, Caldwell and Hayward (1998) report that hospitals have undergone much more substantial change in the last 100 years than school districts have.

Not only is change more dynamic and interactive today, the public expectations for all social service agencies, including schools, have been transformed. Every public service agency is increasingly focused on results, and every agency is being asked to provide better results with constant or even declining fiscal resources. Although various political leaders frame different variations on the theme of higher results from limited resources, the underlying theme itself is increasingly dominant both in this country and in other countries as well.

School districts, like other public organizations, will be moving to a new partnership between the central office and the local school in keeping with the increased pace of change in the world and the new focus on better student performance results coupled with limited fiscal resources. Lawler (1996) has been studying restructured organizations in both the public and the private sectors, especially those involved in "knowledge work," such as schools. He discusses the importance of aligning different dimensions of the organization such as people, purposes, structures, processes, and resources in the service of the organization's key results.

A restructured school district will include a new partnership between the district office and the school. The new partnership has several key themes:

- Districts define student performance standards and collect information about student performance vis-à-vis these standards.
- Districts manage the policy coherence and systemic change process needed in the dynamic new world of education, in-

cluding new results-driven collaboration with community service agencies and families.

- Districts create a new partnership between the district office and the schools that features a shorter and clearer line of authority to schools and much stronger support services to schools under new ground rules.

- Schools have much greater responsibility, authority, and flexibility to help all students reach district-defined performance results.

- Districts and schools have stronger accountability within the new partnership.

In short, the district must shift from being driven by rules to being driven by results, and the district must shift from micromanaging everything in the district to giving schools more authority, responsibility, and accountability for achieving those results.

In proposing a new district-school partnership, we draw extensively on the experiences of the Edmonton public school system in Alberta, Canada (Marsh, 1995). During the 22 years that Mike Strembitsky was the superintendent, this was the most interesting example of the new partnership between the district office and the schools in North America. The unique restructuring approach of the Edmonton public schools, which has approximately 76,000 students in 200 K-12 schools, was built on a districtwide educational foundation. The district defined what students should learn, how success in the district should be assessed, and how the restructuring effort should be organized. There was a districtwide focus on student results, coupled with a dramatic decentralization of authority and resources to schools to help students achieve those results. The experiences in Edmonton provide some valuable guiding principles regarding the general approach to restructuring and the role of the district in relation to schools.

Defining Performance Standards
and a Common Vision

Throughout this book, we have made a case for a new approach to secondary education that begins with identifying a set of common, high expectations for student performance. These common standards, focusing on what students should know and be able to do, form the foundation for the curriculum and instructional program and help all students achieve a basic level of mastery needed for success in future endeavors.

As described in Chapter 4, "Rethinking Curriculum and Instruction in the New American High School," we believe the development of such an integrated system built around these standards requires that the standards be common to all schools in a particular community or state. It is difficult and impractical for each school site to develop its own standards and assessments. Besides, too much variability in student performance standards across schools within the same district or state defeats the purpose of establishing a consistent, coherent set of expectations that has meaning to the community and can be assessed in a way that ensures accountability for results. The need to set standards at a central level points to a powerful imperative for districts to do the following:

- Develop an inclusive process involving the entire community in the establishment of common student performance standards in core subject areas, and
- Use state standards when available or required, or other sources such as New Standards (1997) or professional subject-matter associations, as guidelines for this work.

The district is also responsible for establishing an overall vision for education in its schools that is adopted by the district's governing board. This vision describes the basic philosophy of the school district and provides general direction for attaining the district's major goals. The vision should be broader than the content and performance standards established for student learning and may include noninstructional goals as well. But student performance standards should be the heart of the overall district vision.

In the restructuring of the Edmonton public school system, the district established clear and powerful goals for education and guiding principles for management processes within the district. These goals and principles constituted the core values of the district and guided many types of decisions. The policy documents for the district began with a set of goals that included:

- Developing competencies in reading, writing, speaking, listening, and viewing
- Acquiring basic knowledge, skills, and attitudes in core subjects, referenced to national and international standards
- Acquiring knowledge, skills, attitudes, and habits that contribute to physical, mental, and social well-being
- Developing key attributes of good citizenship at local, national, and international levels
- Acquiring the knowledge, skills, attitudes, and habits required to respond to the opportunities and expectations of the working world

The Edmonton view was that achievement of the broader goals of education was a responsibility shared with the community stakeholders. For example, community influences, of which the home was seen as the most important, must work collaboratively with schools to develop key student characteristics such as intellectual curiosity, the ability to get along with people from diverse backgrounds, and a sense of community responsibility.

The district also established a set of guiding principles for its management processes that consisted of criteria for implementation of the district's strategic plan and its principles of organization. These goals and principles for management, which were written and approved by the school board, focused the role of the district on a result-oriented pathway.

Managing a Results Focus
With Data Support and Policy Coherence

The heart of the new district-school partnership is a strong focus on student results. This results-oriented concept is the cornerstone of the district's educational philosophy and permeates every aspect of the district's operations. The district must work hard to define results indicators and improvement targets, gather results data, and actively use this information to make decisions.

Results should focus on both customer satisfaction and student performance. Districts can elicit input via annual surveys to allow central office staff, school site staff, the community, and students to rate their satisfaction with the district. The results of these surveys are then shared with the public and various stakeholders. In addition, the satisfaction surveys push the principal to find ways to involve teachers, parents, and other stakeholders in the local improvement process.

In recent years, districts have placed considerable emphasis on benchmark achievement exams for students. These benchmark exams might be administered to students in grades 4, 8, and 10 in the core subject areas to determine student performance levels. Underlying this view of benchmarked student achievement is the idea that the curriculum should be aligned with results expected of the student. In many districts, curriculum is centralized as a district responsibility and instruction is decentralized as a school and teaching responsibility. Districts carry out benchmarking in another sense—searching worldwide to find the best programs that help students learn in priority learning areas. For example, districts are benchmarking their early literacy programs to the best practices in the world, and have found programs that far exceed local practices and local expectations about what is possible in a learning environment.

To help support schools with an emphasis on results, districts need to transform their testing office into a standards-driven office of student information and to monitor student performance in a way that is very client centered. By gathering information and compiling reports, the district office provides critical information for monitoring priorities within a given school, evaluating school satisfaction with district priorities, and preparing strategies to help schools improve.

Every district will need a new way of operating in this results-driven system. Everyone in the district will need to be clear about the student performance standards that really matter. Unfortunately, some districts have adopted not one but multiple sets of standards that meet the needs of various state and federal agencies, and this only creates confusion about what goals students, teachers, and district leaders have.

Every district will also need a data management system tied to the student performance standards. The system must provide quality student performance data that meet the program improvement and status reporting needs. We have found that a balance of on-demand tests linked with indicators of student writing such as writing portfolios is the best solution in meeting the needs of both internal and external audiences.

Every district will also need leaders who focus on the student performance data and lead improvement efforts linked to these result indicators. The focus will need to be relentless and deep in the culture of the district for schools and students to be effective. We need district-wide inquiry and collaboration on these matters: a learning community driven by student results.

To help schools and students achieve the district's vision and standards, the role of the district office needs to be reexamined to align structures and services with the new educational orientation. Districts need to ensure that all the decisions they make—about the curriculum, budget, policies, collective bargaining agreement, staffing, professional development, and any other district service—lead toward the desired student results. This is policy coherence at the most critical level.

Finally, districts need to determine which of these decisions can be delegated to school sites to provide sufficient latitude for schools to tailor their programs to meet student needs. Districts may set the standards, but they do not need to have sole control over the implementation of those standards. Because the world is dynamic and constantly changing, the district leadership in setting priorities and aligning decisions and organizational structures to those priorities will be ongoing and demanding. The best districts will be good managers of the change process related to a standards-based school system.

Reframing the Partnership Between the District and the School

Are decentralized decisions better than centralized ones? The answer is best framed as which decisions should be centralized and which decentralized. We have already discussed some key decisions that need to be centralized: decisions about choosing the student performance standards and performance indicators, managing the data collection process, providing policy coherence that supports student results, and managing the complex change process of the new partnership. We can now look at which decisions should be decentralized and how the system should hang together. The new partnership needs new arrangements for authority, service, and accountability between the district and the school.

Reframing the Authority Arrangements in the Partnership

An essential element in the systemic support for the new high school is the restructuring of the relationship between the district and the school in a way that gives schools considerable programmatic authority and resources for achieving results. Reframing the partnership between the district and schools must be guided by the belief that accountability must come first and authority must follow. Districts must carefully avoid mandating the means schools use to reach results; schools must give highest priority to getting the job of education done by producing results. Even though districts define what constitutes student results, schools are left to their own creative inventions on how to obtain these results. Reframing this authority in the new partnership includes the following elements.

School Leaders Need Only One Boss in the District Office

A guiding principle must be that every employee should have only one boss; the new partnership hinges on the school-district version of this idea. Many school principals are left with the often accurate impression that everyone in the district office is their boss, with the ability to make extensive demands on their time. The partnership fails if this pattern persists. Nothing signals the reframed partnership better than the sorting of out-of-line authority and service arrangements in the system. Everyone needs a line of authority that is short and clear; that can authorize "yes" decisions as readily as "no" decisions; and that can focus all the key components of effectiveness on the student results targets.

A Clear Locus of Authority at the School Site

Authority for program design and resource allocation at the site level rests with the school principal, rather than with a vaguely defined collaborative mechanism. Principals use a variety of strategies to engage staff and the community in decision making about program design and resource allocation in relation to the expected results defined by the district, but the principal is the clear locus of authority at the school site and is held accountable.

Development of School Improvement Plans

Principals are responsible for preparing annual school plans that set improvement targets for student learning and program operations and that link program design and resource allocation to these targets. These plans will be quite different from the usual school reform plans currently found in our high schools. Unfortunately, most current plans have a fuzzy picture of the student performance improvement targets that are the heart of the new plans (see the discussion of the new school plans in Chapter 7, "A New High School Design Focused on Student Performance"). Most school plans also reflect a fragmented and piece-meal view of the needed modifications to the school; our view of school design calls for much more coherent and robust school reforms. But most important, current school plans are a wish list that can be refreshed without real consequences each year. On the one hand, schools have not had the flexibility and authority to make real change; on the other hand, no one has held them accountable for the success of their reforms. What a mess.

In the new partnership between districts and schools, school boards spend their time monitoring student progress and seeing if the school plans lead to student performance success. Districts approve the school plans and may negotiate with the school about improvement targets, but school leaders are given considerable latitude in determining how to achieve the desired results.

Distribution of Resources to the School Site

In many high schools today, principals are responsible for many budgets because of the awkward and dysfunctional way funding is provided to schools. The new partnership requires a funding alloca-tion formula that integrates budgets and focuses resource allocation to the school, and within the school, toward student results. For this, districts need to maximize financial resources at the site level by shifting a very high percentage of the financial resources to the schools. Districts and states also need to shift the way equity concerns are handled in schools. The new focus should be on whether all students are learning up to standard rather than what funding and which services are provided to students with special needs. The equity concerns in the new high school must focus on student performance results—that is the key to any student's future.

Principals need to be given considerable latitude in defining how resources are spent to achieve the desired results within their schools. Principals in many other countries have this expanded latitude and use it to shift resources among all the line items of the budget. Principals also need more flexibility from certain state regulations, which severely hinder local creativity in many cases. But the goal is not fewer rules; it is greater student performance.

In addition, schools need incentives to generate additional resources. For instance, principals who design innovative and unique programs and can attract additional financial support and resources to the school should be able to retain those resources at the site. This policy provides sites with a major incentive to be both effective and cost-efficient.

Expansion of Principals' Roles

Schools need principals who act as instructional leaders with the resources and authority to provide overall direction for instruction. Schools also need principals who are accountable for achieving the improvement targets in the school plans. This new combination of authority and accountability frames the strategic instructional role of the principal. Teachers often report feeling more empowered under this arrangement because they have a principal with the authority to implement proposals that can help enhance school performance results. Teachers like to know who can say "yes" to important proposals.

Expansion of Teachers' Roles

In standards-based high schools, many teachers have major opportunities for leadership and professional development within the school. In Chapter 7, "A New High School Design Focused on Student Performance," we describe a house structure that allows a team of teachers to work with a group of students over most of the school day. This high-performance work team has many key elements of collaboration and authority essential to student performance success. Teachers also must play a key role in the schoolwide management of the school; this new form of standards-centered site-based management has been successful in business and public organizations.

Reframing Service and Support to Schools

The district office and the schools are connected by line authority and service relationships. In the new partnership, the central office is accountable for providing quality services and the schools are accountable for achieving student learning results. Several features make this arrangement successful. The organization chart of the district must reflect the dramatic difference between the line authority and support service roles of the district office and a culture that supports a very strong service orientation must be built.

But a change in the district's organization chart isn't enough. Edmonton leaders found that when the fiscal resources were shifted to schools, school leaders could purchase the services they needed rather than just receive the services the district bureaucracy felt the schools needed. This shift in the control of resources meant that school leaders now could decide which support services would make the greatest contribution to the school's achievement of student results. What an effective way to build a stronger customer service culture within the district. In Edmonton, shifting the funding for services to the school site prompted the district photocopy center to change its customer service orientation and effectiveness.

But schools need choice in where to obtain their support services—district offices are not and should not be the only providers. Instead, the central office needs to compete for the school's business in the open marketplace against outside vendors. Schools need control of the services coming to them; after all, schools are accountable for the student results the services must support. So schools need the resources and authority to buy the services that will best help them meet their performance goals. They also need a district that focuses on the results, but lets the schools decide how best to accomplish those results.

In Edmonton, school leaders had the funds to purchase curriculum consultant services from the district office, from private consultants, or from regional service centers. School leaders purchased the services they felt would have the greatest effect on student performance. In turn, consultants could work with schools that really wanted the consultant services. The district could also buy some consultant time to meet district priorities and managed the scheduling of the consultants.

The central office in Edmonton supported schools in other ways as well. The district provided workshops for aspiring school principals and accelerated the career path of promising candidates. The district also worked hard to identify, develop, and retain effective principals, and careful attention was given to supporting good principals and replacing weaker ones.

The district office also provided district leaders who coached school principals. The Edmonton district had seven associate superintendents who each were responsible for approximately 30 schools. Their primary function was to help mentor or coach school principals, set improvement targets, assist in school plans, facilitate team planning, and provide a clear vision of district expectations. When the school was not meeting its responsibilities for achieving student success, the role of the district coach shifted toward greater line authority.

Ensuring Accountability for Student Results in the New Partnership

Accountability in the new American high school is built into all organizational levels and shared by everyone involved in a student's education. The district must play a unique role in establishing an effective accountability system and in communicating student results to the community it serves, however (Tucker & Codding, 1995). Information about student performance and progress toward district goals is also essential to make decisions about the effectiveness of programs, resource allocation, and staff.

Several accountability themes are essential in the new American high school. Accountability is an important link between the district that set the standards and the school that must now help students reach those standards. The key themes include the following.

1. The accountability system is based on student performance standards associated with the Certificate of Initial Mastery (CIM). In a standards-based system, the student and the school-level performance indicators are clear, public, and important, as described in Chapter 3, "Standards and Assessment." Without such a credible assessment system, the accountability strategy becomes illusive and unsustainable as teachers are left to develop their own individual methods of evaluating student performance. When there is a standards-based assessment system, the evaluation of the teaching and

learning process includes a common perspective. Students know they must work toward a quality standard shared by the professional staff. Teachers know that their peers are watching—the results of their practice are subjected to the scrutiny of colleagues. This makes the school a good place to work for those who produce results and uncomfortable for those who do not. But public scrutiny for both students and teachers is necessary to ensure accountability for results.

2. Both the school and the students are accountable for achieving this high level of student performance. The school is accountable for having an increasingly large percentage of students reach the CIM. In Kentucky, for example, a performance index score is calculated for each school, and that score becomes the baseline for its student performance improvement targets in core academic subjects. Schools are held accountable in comparison to their unique baseline, which levels the playing field and focuses accountability on the value the school adds to student performance.

But having all students focused on achieving the CIM provides student as well as school accountability. The CIM pushes all students to high performance levels and makes the criteria for student success very clear. It also makes the accountability very fair. When the school, not the student, is accountable, teachers often wonder why they are seen as the only source of accountability and why they alone must make the learning successful.

3. Accountability, authority, and responsibility go together. When the school is accountable, it also needs control of resources and authority to achieve success. This leads to the question, Who at the school is accountable for the school meeting its improvement targets on the CIM and similar indicators? Here opinions split into two camps. Some districts, such as Edmonton, hold a single person—the principal—accountable. The principal has the line authority link to the district and can engage the school community in helping all students reach high performance levels. In other jurisdictions, a formally constituted school council is the locus of authority, responsibility, and accountability. To date, however, it has been hard to find an enduring and successful example of this group responsibility model. But a fundamental lesson is clear: The person or group must have the authority and stability to make key decisions, must have the obliga-

tion to see them through, and must be unambiguously accountable for their results. Conversely, what clearly does not work is governance by an amorphous community that is not responsible, accountable, nor often even present over time.

4. The accountability system includes both incentives and sanctions. Incentives play a key role in all our lives. Currently, in high schools, the incentives arrangements are a mess for both students and teachers. As discussed in Chapter 1, "Just Passing Through," students have little incentive to work hard and achieve at high levels, and teachers have little authority and incentive to ensure that students are performing at their best.

With the CIM, students have a certificate that matters to themselves, their peers, their school, and their future. The CIM can help build a success-oriented culture where effort matters and the criteria for success are clear. For the system to work, however, teachers and schools also need incentives for success. We emphasize an approach to incentives that is based on student performance, that provides both intrinsic and extrinsic motivation to teachers, and that allows incentives to be earned by the team or school, but gives incentives to each teacher. In Kentucky, for example, teachers at a school can earn a group reward for strong student improvement based on the school's unique baseline. Teachers at the school can then decide to use the money for school improvement efforts or as a bonus for each individual teacher. We favor the bonus to teachers as part of a new type of salary schedule that rewards strong student performance rather than teacher longevity.

But standards-based accountability needs school sanctions as well as school rewards. Sanctions fit with the moral view that failure will not be tolerated for America's youth. The sanctions should be based on a set of phases of external intervention triggered by student performance results at the school. First, schools need a signal that their students' performance is not acceptable and that a stronger plan for improvement is required. An external probation manager should be asked to approve the school's plan and guide the improvement process.

If the poor performance persists, the next stage of intervention is triggered. This stage may lead to reconstitution of the school, including possible dismissal of school leaders or teachers. The goal is to have all students succeed.

In short, an effective accountability system is based on clearly defined standards and goals centered on student performance, provides relevant and useful data about success in reaching those standards, and can be used by school staff as well as district staff and board members to make decisions and improve practices. It connects authority, responsibility, and accountability—one cannot exist without the others. It also provides incentives for students as well as the system, and clearly defined sanctions for sustained poor performance. In a standards-based system, accountability is not an afterthought; it is a necessity.

9

Some Tough Choices Ahead

David D. Marsh

EVERY HIGH SCHOOL student will need a high-powered education to succeed in the 21st century. Every student will need a deep understanding of key concepts, and the ability to apply these in solving problems in their homes, their jobs, and their society. They will need strong character and interpersonal skills as well. They all must "think for a living" to create a just and prosperous society. As a society, we must establish these goals for our schools, and without delay.

This chapter has two parts: a synthesis of the proposal for the new American high school and a preview of the tough choices that we face if we are to have all students reach high standards. Only in making the tough choices and forming the moral imperative for this work will we succeed.

The New American High School:
A Synthesis

The current comprehensive high school will not help all our students reach a high level of student performance. The comprehensive high school concept may have been a good idea when just over half of America's teenagers completed high school 40 years ago. It is emphatically not the right idea for America now, when we expect almost all our youth to qualify for the certificate of initial mastery (CIM).

Building on James Conant's (1959) proposal for the comprehensive high school in the 1950s, American high schools currently have so many priorities that they are the masters of none. They dilute learning with an endless array of poorly articulated goals, when they need a set of clear and compelling student performance standards. They are driven by rules and regulations, when they need to be driven by student performance results. They focus on curriculum coverage, when they need to focus on what students have learned from that curriculum. They encourage passive participation, when accountable action and strong incentives for success are needed. They encourage the sorting of students into self-fulfilling predictions of varied student performance, when relentless persistence to see that all students have learned is a better moral choice and a feasible pedagogical approach. They alienate and distract students, when they should engage and support students and draw on the strengths of the community context for student learning.

The direction we propose responds to the significant problems in our current high schools. No individual person or group is at fault for these problems; instead, we see the problems as being deeply rooted in the current design of our schools and school systems. In turn, like many people across the country, we see real and lasting promise in the directions emerging across America.

In this book, we have proposed a new approach to high school education. Our proposal is centered on the CIM, a certificate of student performance expected of all students by age 16. The CIM represents what all students need to know and be able to do in core academic subjects such as English language arts, math, science, and history. The CIM is the standard for all students, not just honors students, and should be benchmarked to the performance levels of the best educational efforts in the world. We think this level of student performance is a moral imperative for our students and our nation. This level of performance is also within our collective grasp given a new design for the American high school.

Our new design is grounded in student performance standards, like those of New Standards (1997). Standards are quite new to secondary education in America, although other countries have designed and implemented graduation-by-performance systems for some time. We can do even better than other countries when states or districts create clear and credible standards that define not only what is important to learn (the content standards), but also how good is good enough (the performance standards). These performance standards must be concrete—the standards must be accompanied by examples of student work that do and do not meet the standards and by commentary on why the piece of work did or did not meet the standard. Such a grounded view of what is important to learn would be very helpful to teachers, students, parents, school and system leaders, and the community.

A standards-based assessment system and a powerful learning environment must be connected to the standards. The assessment system must include both ongoing assessment of student learning that could guide the next phase of instruction, and end-of-course exams, on-demand reference exams, and culminating projects that provide a more intense assessment of what students have learned over a period of time. With this assessment, we can finally have a uniform grading system—a system where grades are linked to standards and have uniform performance standards across teachers and schools. The assessment system must be linked to a management information approach that generates useful and accessible information for multiple audiences so that results can drive student learning, instruction, and accountability.

Our redesigned American high schools also need a coherent and powerful curriculum. When the curriculum flows from the standards and is solidly based on the academic core subjects, then everyone can focus on what really matters: student results. The curriculum should be organized around a few key concepts and skills done in depth each year. In this model, each course has a new type of syllabus that shows the game plan for the year linked to the standards for the course.

Teachers need other tools to help students learn. We have proposed a new set of instructional tools to replace the dysfunctional textbook in American schools. Our tools include a concept book that lets students focus on the key ideas underlying each course, paired with problem-solving and skill books to provide high-quality practice. Another key tool is a set of core assignments—major projects and units that generate the engaging and powerful student work linked to student performance standards for the course. The learning environment must also provide multiple access points for the curriculum, which we call "on-ramps," and powerful catch-up strategies triggered by frequent analysis of standards-related student work.

For student learning to be successful, we need a new school design. We began our view of the school design with student performance standards, and then showed the range of school components that must be aligned with the standards. We talked about the need for a safe and clean environment for everyone at the school as the base from which real learning can take place. Surrounding the curriculum and learning expectations must be incentives for all students to take tough courses and work hard. Success also requires a school climate and organizational structures that provide strong personal support for each student. Every student needs an adult in the school who acts on the belief that the student can and will succeed. This approach to student empowerment is linked to student success—the only type of empowerment that will help in the long run. The new American high school also needs a strong culture that focuses relentlessly on results and getting every student to achieve the standards.

High schools will also need reform in school organization, management, and governance. The goal is that each of these is focused on achieving student results and reinforces the expectation that every student is expected to reach high standards. The organization, management, and governance must also make clear what each member of the school community will be held accountable for with respect to that goal. At the same time, standards-oriented high schools require school leadership that is inclusive, making everyone, including staff, students, and parents, feel that they are welcome participants in the drive to improve results.

But schools cannot be successful working in isolation. Everyone at the school must work to build links to community services and supports for students outside of school so that they are able to take full advantage of school. In this book, we have described how schools must also help parents engage more directly in helping their own children's success in school.

Schools cannot make these changes without a new partnership with school systems. We believe that this new partnership will work best when the central administration defines what is to be learned and holds schools accountable for achieving those results. This arrangement then shifts much greater authority, responsibility, and accountability to schools for achieving those results. Simultaneously, the central administration must relinquish its habit of directing every aspect of school improvement.

Making the Tough Choices

Creating the new American high school is a challenging but important mission. It requires some tough choices for school and system leaders, students, parents, and the American public. First, it will require a commitment to the view that all students can and must perform to a high and common standard. One key component of this commitment is the view that ability and hard work lead to success. Our country was founded on the belief that hard work leads to success. And it has.

But in American schools, this expectation has become confounded by competing paradigms. On the one hand, America pioneered the development of the common school where students from all walks of life could learn. On the other hand, we also promoted the "ability" view of student success—some students have ability and therefore can succeed at whatever level they choose, whereas others do not have it and therefore have to limit their expectations. Early in this century, we developed major testing efforts that sorted out students seen as having academic ability from those without it. This negative, ability-based design led to one of the most tracked secondary school systems in the modern world. Research and experience confirm that effort rather than ability is most related to student success in almost every area. Students and their teachers who work very hard and share a belief that all students can learn have dramatic success.

Another component of the commitment to all students is the view that all students can learn to a very high level, as is found in some other countries. Whatever one's perspective about how well our students have performed to date, the perspective for the 21st century must be that all students can and must perform much better than has been the case in this country. Some countries have an effort-based view of learning, and have established policies and practices that narrow the performance gap between high-performing and low-performing schools. When America used its compensatory education funds to support programs designed to lift the achievement of all students, we also were immensely successful in narrowing the range while raising the level of performance of our students.

Acting on the belief that all students can and must learn is a moral issue. Leaders in our schools and school systems must join with community leaders and policymakers to anchor our reforms in this belief. Acting on this belief will move us past issues of race and poverty as predictors of student achievement; the answer is that all students can learn if we act powerfully on the belief that they can.

School leaders have some tough choices to make in creating and acting on the belief that all students can learn. They must move past easy rhetoric, using a strong approach to personal learning and an action agenda. To build the collective culture, the individual leader must first be transformed. This personal transformation will require reflection and soul-searching, and a careful look at one's own current practice in the school. Then school leaders need to look at data about student results and be ready to ask hard questions about beliefs as well as practices. Hard questions require tough choices. For leaders to decide to open up issues of belief that all students can learn will require a tough decision about strategy and direction.

Some tough choices include:

- How will you insist that all students complete demanding classes in core subjects? What will be required? How will that requirement be enforced?
- How will you build and maintain the political support for the policy and practice that all students will succeed? How will you insist on this priority with students, guidance counselors, teachers, parents, school board members, and the public at large?
- What will you do when academic priorities clash with social or athletic priorities in the school?

A second challenge is creating a standards-driven system that matches the view that all students can and must learn to a very high standard. Five years ago, this challenge would have been seriously delayed by a lack of credible student standards, a lack of viable assessment strategies, and a lack of powerful instructional strategies linked to those standards. Fortunately, in the last 5 years, much progress has been made. Extensive work has been done by New Standards (1997) and many states to create promising examples of student content standards. National opinion polls show strong support among public school teachers and students for standards as the focus of high schools. But the journey is only half finished.

Now we must move forward to complete the design and implementation of the CIM. The states are establishing the content standards that identify what should be learned. The CIM itself will establish the system that formalizes the performance level required of all students. Establishing the CIM will require addressing the complex issues of priorities, resource trade-offs, and policy changes and policy stability needed for its success. If we are serious about high school reform, we must embrace the heart of the new standards-based reform—the CIM.

The CIM could be a national certificate, or it could be a national concept that is formalized in a state-specific version of the CIM certificate. In any case, the certificate represents the core academic knowledge needed by all students before they launch into serious technical or college preparation. The certificate would go a long way toward focusing reform efforts on student results and aligning policies and practices around it. It would also provide meaningful leverage for job hunting or entry into various levels of schooling prior to entering the workforce.

School leaders will have some tough choices to make while implementing a standards-driven focus at their schools. In many schools, the standards system is a glass only half full. School leaders must see and act on the view that the glass is half full, rather than half empty. The editors of this book have been strongly encouraged in seeing how far the standards-based reform has come in just a few years. But some will see the glass as half empty and express concern that others are to blame for the mess.

Building a standards-based culture and approach at each high school is possible. It will require some tough choices about how to build the culture, how to internalize and refine the jurisdiction's direction, and how to monitor student success in ways that enhance student learning.

Some tough choices include:

- What are the core purposes at your school? What criteria will you use to see that the purposes are accomplished?
- Will you make the tough choices about a focus on the CIM or will you continue to be all things to all people as was proposed in the comprehensive high school?

- How will you launch a CIM at your school or district? Will it truly have an internationally-benchmarked standard?
- How will the CIM drive everything at the school?
- What happens to the high school diploma?
- What happens to social promotion into high school? Are you ready to establish a gateway assessment that determines entrance into high school? How will you resolve the many issues this gateway assessment is linked to?
- Are you really ready to make the standard the constant factor and time the variable factor when our current practice has these in the opposite order of priority?

A final challenge is to do whatever it takes to help all students reach a very high level of student performance and have powerful incentives and accountability for that accomplishment. Imagine that the CIM has been established as a national or state-level certificate required of all students. Now high school and community leaders must work to create a learning environment equal to the task of helping all students learn to this high level. Earlier in this book, we describe the program and organizational components that we believe will be needed. To establish these components will require strong leadership at the school and system level. Leaders will need a relentless drive to help all students succeed, and the information support to help this happen. This mission has both technological and cultural dimensions, but ultimately it is a problem of willpower and creativity. Each school needs to be a learning community driven by student results, with a collective commitment to helping all students succeed on the CIM as the moral force behind the effort.

Creating a learning community driven by results will require some tough choices for school leaders. Many aspects of the current high school do not fit with the new direction for the school, and will need to be dramatically overhauled. A tension is needed in the learning community—a tension between comfort and support of teachers and students and the pressing need for dramatic improvement in student performance. School leaders have important decisions to make about how to maintain ownership and professional growth of teachers while insisting on strong student performance improvement.

Leaders need to realize that everyone on the team is a potential asset. Teachers expect hard work from students; students require the support of parents and extended family members; and families can count on the support of communities and the school. Although this teamwork has a foundation in organizational and policy support, in the end, individual effort will matter now that the focus on student performance is clear. But because schools don't work like this, school leaders have some tough decisions to make about how to build this team approach.

The accountability and incentives must also be clear and consistent. It is easy to talk about accountability and incentives; it is another thing to make the system work and carry through with the tough decisions. Our high schools currently are flush with multiple priorities and champions of those priorities. We will need to stop doing some things, even interesting things, so that the academic core can be tied to student results. We will also need to focus scarce resources and energy as incentives that matter to students. Employers, universities, and technical institutions must care about the performance criteria at which we want students to excel. Otherwise, the message to students will again be garbled. We have a lot of work to do.

Accountability for results has had an awkward history in education. We increasingly have the technology for assessing important student performance, and will create even better assessment approaches in the years to come. What will matter more in the next millennium will be a fair accountability system that asks for strong and successful effort from schools and students, provides for positive growth, and also provides serious sanctions for failing schools. This approach to accountability requires changes in rules and privileges, professional orientation, and skilled leadership.

It will be hard to make significant improvement in the lives of our youth if they do not share the belief in student results and the accountability for these results. The CIM puts the responsibility for student achievement jointly on the shoulders of the individual student and the learning environment. With a clear and sensible set of learning goals, with assessment that is common and fair, and with incentives for students as well as the school, the vision of the new American high school can become a reality. But the high school will need a new partnership with the system.

Some tough choices include:

- How will your school find the worldwide best programs linked to the required standards, and how will you make sure these are implemented in the best ways?
- How will you make sure that everything in the school is focused on the CIM? How will you deal with the counter-pressure to give every subject and teacher an equal portion of the "goodies" whether they are essential to the CIM or not? What about your school must be discontinued and how will you do that?
- How will you support, and insist on, the teacher development needed to make the standards-driven high school succeed?

Some Hard Decisions for State and District Leadership

Moving forward will require some hard choices for state and district leaders as well. The problem is not one of just getting the system off the back of the school and the student. We already have a system that strongly influences schools and students. Instead, state and district leaders should establish the policy context for the transformation of the high school. Many aspects of standards-based reform will require bold, positive policy coherence.

Creating a Standards-Based Certificate System

Selecting the standards will be difficult—there are many important concepts and skills that students could learn. The system will be challenged to create a process that identifies what knowledge and skills will be vital for the 21st century. This process must be sufficiently inclusive to gain widespread acceptance—but the ultimate test will be whether the concepts and skills provide a powerful focus for learning.

Another tough decision will be to create one stable set of standards. Many state and district leaders are working on many reform efforts, and each seems to have its own set of standards. Helping school leaders understand the interrelationship among the multiple sets of standards won't do—every state and district needs a simpler and clearer message of what is important to learn.

Finally, just a set of standards, even performance standards, won't be sufficient if it is not tied to a certificate system such as the CIM. States and districts must give both students and high schools the message that the standards must be met. Going beyond the rhetoric of a results focus to a certificate system will require both political will and careful design. If the certificate isn't clearly linked to technical and academic pathways beyond high school, it will not make enough difference—that design issue will require new governance arrangements in most states and some important agreements that give students reason to work hard.

Some tough choices include:

- How will your district or state define the essential CIM standards?
- Will you include the "new" basics of conceptual understanding, or will you settle for only the "old basics" as California has done in mathematics?
- Will the CIM be for all students, or only a student elite?
- What certificate system and pathways to further professional and technical education are tied to the CIM?
- What time frame are you willing to follow, or will the CIM only be dangled as a promise to schools and students?

Linking the Appropriate Assessment to the
Performance Standards That Underlie the Certificate System

Tough decisions also await those who create the assessment system linked to the performance standards. The assessment must serve several purposes—careful judgments about the accomplishments of each student and guidance to many groups about how to improve learning. Such assessment systems are expensive to build, and require collaboration across many role groups. But they can be built, as has been demonstrated in countries with effective educational systems.

A strong information system must surround the assessment system, and this information system faces both technical and political challenges. Leaders must decide on questions of access, cost sharing, hardware, and software. It will be even more difficult to create effective utilization. Fortunately, there are many exemplars for most aspects of the information system, but a culture and system must be created that support high performance, not just more visible high risk.

Some tough choices include:

- Will your district or state be willing to invest in or adopt a high-quality performance assessment system such as the one New Standards has developed, or will the assessment be based only on existing standardized tests that capture only a small portion of the essential standards?
- Are you really committed to a criterion-based system where all students can potentially do very well, or are you still committed to a norm-referenced assessment system where half the students will be "below average" on some fuzzy standard?

Creating Powerful Curriculum and Instructional Programs
That Help All Students Reach the Certificate

The power and integration of the best instructional programs far surpass what most teachers are able to design on their own. But good teachers are vital to the success of any program. Balancing inclusive planning and professional development with strong program design will require strong leadership and careful work.

Getting textbook publishers to help solve the new curriculum problems will also require strong leadership. When states and major school districts create a stable set of standards, especially standards common across jurisdictions, they can create the basis for textbook companies to delimit and focus their materials. In turn, standards-based textbooks and curriculum tools support student learning. Creating this new partnership between system leaders and textbook companies is vital to the success of the transformed high school.

Some tough choices include:

- Will your district or state be willing to adopt and create instructional materials that focus directly on the core standards of the CIM?

- Will you be willing to insist on this focus, and not adopt or use instructional materials that are "a mile wide and an inch deep" in focus?
- How will effective programs—the best in the world—be found and made available to schools?
- What system support will be needed to ensure that students "catch up" and succeed in earning the CIM?

Shifting From a "Regulations" to a "Results" Focus
as the Basis of Systemic Direction for High Schools

Here is the Achilles' heel for high school reform in most states and districts. The systems can identify and hold schools accountable for high student performance, but if school leaders must respond to a wide and often disjointed set of rules, regulations, and resource allocation formulas, the reforms will not work. The decisions are especially tough because the system itself must clearly change if the school is to change.

Systems must find a way to integrate categorical programs in support of the standards. They must review every aspect of the regulatory education code in the state or district, and create a results-driven code instead. In this process of system redirection, many traditional interests will be challenged, many people will need to change, and a major new culture will need to be built.

Some tough choices include:

- What regulations stand in the way of schools being responsible and accountable for student success, and how will the whole set of regulations be changed to support school authority and accountability for student learning?
- How will schools get the control of fiscal and human resources needed to make their accountability meaningful?
- How will authority, responsibility, and accountability be integrated at the system and the school level?
- How will you keep the district and state restructuring moving forward? It won't work if only the school is asked to make the significant changes.

Creating an Accountability System That
Supports and Matters to Schools and Students

It has been easy to identify "poor-performing schools" using traditional measures. It will be more challenging to identify a standards-based accountability system that uses performance standards and good assessment as the basis for viewing "strong-performing" schools. Schools and students need real incentives, and these cost money. There will be tough choices about generating the funding, and also about choosing to use the money for incentives to schools and students. There will be tough choices about how to help poor-performing schools when the schools have been unable to improve themselves—choices about effective intervention, allocation of responsibility and authority, and criteria for success.

But there will also be tough choices about what to do when poor performing schools ultimately don't improve. Currently, most states and districts do not have the levers or the strategies to hold poor performing schools accountable. The threat of takeover has had little substance. Every state and district will need serious discussion about this issue, and every jurisdiction will need levers and strategies if all schools and all students are to improve.

Some tough choices include:

- What benefits will successful schools and students enjoy? Can they count on these benefits?
- What system support will you need to provide to sustain this incentive strategy? Are the incentives for school and student success really that powerful? What should you do to ensure that the incentives are truly powerful?
- What consequences and sanctions will be in force for students and schools? Why should they believe that these sanctions will matter, when previous proposals often were not carried out?

In short, districts and states must create policy coherence that actually helps every school and every student succeed. The future of our nation rests on this shared work. We must go forward. To insist on the old priorities and practices is simply immoral.

Epilogue
Anne's World—circa 2005

Marc S. Tucker
Judy B. Codding

ANNE HAD BEEN on the stage under the hot lights for two hours straight, but she was not tired. She had the mounting feeling of exhilaration that, in recent years, she always had when she was handing out diplomas at graduation. And then she saw Debbie Williams standing diffidently at the bottom of the stairs, waiting to step up to the stage, and her heart took a great leap.

It was Debbie and the other students like her that made it all—the trauma, the conflicts, the seven-day weeks—worthwhile. There was no doubt at all about it. If Debbie had been a senior's age five years ago, she would not have been in this line. She would not have been in school. She would have dropped out and hit the streets long ago. For sure.

This young woman mounting the stairs with pride and self-assurance had no memory of her father. Her mother had been sick and unable to work most of her adult life. Debbie, her mom and the other four children had more than once been without a home for long periods. Debbie's older brother had grown into his teenage years scared and full of bravado. He was dead now, gunned down in a gang fight over drugs.

Seven years ago, Debbie would have slipped quietly through the cracks, a cipher in this great big building. She had entered the ninth grade reading with great difficulty, just able to sound out the words in her textbooks, with the vocabulary of a fifth grader, if that. She had a little arithmetic. Her spoken English was highly ungrammatical as measured against the structure of standard English. She sat in her classes apathetic and resentful, knowing she would fail, knowing that all the adults in her life expected her to fail and would do nothing to help her. Now and then, when she gave in to the overwhelming frustration, she would act out and get into instant trouble. It was a race between expulsion and dropping out.

But five years ago, Anne had committed Adams High to revolution. She had persuaded the faculty that they had nowhere to go but up. The district had just adopted its own version of the New Standards Performance Standards. Anne and the faculty decided together that they wanted to lead the way.

There had been some real resentment on the part of the faculty about the district's adoption of the standards. They thought it had all been done for public relations by school board members eager to make election points with the public about the new standards-based accountability system. These teachers saw the adoption of the standards as the leading edge of just another round of teacher-bashing.

But Anne presented it all in a very different light, in a way that was very appealing to most of the faculty. She said it was really a matter of what they owed to these kids and to themselves as professional educators, that this was, after all, what they had all signed up for when they decided on the calling of teacher. Maybe the kids could perform at these levels and maybe they couldn't, but this faculty was going to give it everything they had.

None of it had been easy. When Anne had pointed out that the biggest problem for many of the students entering school was low reading comprehension, most of the English teachers had said they had not been hired to teach reading, they did not know anything about reading and, if reading needed to be taught, Anne would have to hire someone else to do it—outside of the regular school day. That was a bad moment.

But then something interesting had happened. Anne had asked the university to come in to do a careful assessment of the student body's reading level. The results had been appalling. More than half of the student body was reading two or more grades below level, and a substantial number well below that. A rising chorus of faculty members, led by one of the younger English teachers, rose up in a rather dramatic faculty meeting and said, "We cannot avoid this problem any longer. It is affecting performance in every subject in this school." The young turks volunteered to form a study group to see what other high schools had done about this problem and come back to the faculty with some proposals. And they did just that.

In retrospect, Anne thought, that faculty meeting had been the turning point in many ways. The head of the English department retired shortly thereafter. Anne replaced him with the young man who had spoken up at the faculty meeting, who had since steeped himself in the rather slender literature on what was known about teaching reading to young adults. Something similar to this miracle had happened in the math department. They had the leadership they needed in two key spots now and nothing could stop them.

Every week, it seemed, she was asking for volunteers among the faculty to research some problem, find some resource, come up with some plan. One group in each department was analyzing student performance against the standards to see where the students were strong and where they were weak. Another group was researching the ways that schools in other districts across the nation were using extra time before school, after school, during school and on Saturday mornings to help kids who were behind to catch up. It turned out that many of these programs had very disappointing effects, but some were very effective. The study group homed in on the effective practices and made very pointed recommendations as to how to adapt those practices to the specific situation at Adams High School.

And so it went, in one arena after another. In the beginning, most of what they had done was rather serendipitous, like the new reading program. They stumbled on problems, and tried to solve them, in no particular order. Later, they realized that they needed a plan, a way to get a picture of the whole, and then set priorities.

They began to look at the standards as the linchpin of the new system. And, after a seemingly endless debate, which at times got very heated, they decided that they would try to sell the parents, students and community on a radically different design for the structure of the whole school, based on the idea that a student should not be allowed to go from the lower division to the upper division without meeting

a standard of performance that would enable him to begin the freshman year of college without remediation. Many faculty members
thought that was a pipe dream—the students simply could not do it.
Others thought that the students could do it, but that neither the
parents nor the community would let them deny diplomas to students
who could not meet the new—and much higher—standard.

Anne knew the kids could do it, but she was in fact very worried
the community would never go for this new graduation standard. But
she was willing to stake her career on trying for it.

First she put together a planning group consisting of key faculty
members, student leaders, parents and community members to come
up with a detailed plan that she could offer to the school board, with
her superintendent's support. To her surprise, the idea caught on like
wildfire in the business community, who sent some very powerful
business leaders to testify at the school board meeting. Impressed, the
board voted in favor, despite some strong opposition from some
parents who were very worried that, when push came to shove, the
school district would not make the changes needed to give their
children a fair shot at the new diploma standard. Anne listened
carefully to what they had to say, found herself more sympathetic to
their concerns than she had anticipated, and vowed to do everything
she possibly could to prove them wrong, more than anything else
because she realized that her conscience could not take it if numbers
of students started dropping out of school because they thought they
could not meet the new standards, students who would have stayed
and gotten a diploma under the old system. She knew at that board
meeting that a revolution in how her school did business was now the
only option she and the staff had. There was no turning back once the
diploma issue had been decided.

The work had been endless. It often seemed like one step back for
every one taken forward, or was it the other way around? Infinite
rounds of hand-scheduling students and teachers into the new master
schedule after the house system went into effect. Until they got into
the routine of it.

Many arguments about the curriculum—what should be in the
core for the lower division curriculum, what should be an elective and
what could be left out altogether? Fierce partisans of the International
Baccalaureate and equally fierce partisans of the Advanced Placement
System. There were even those who wanted to develop the whole academic program curriculum from scratch, though they were quickly

voted down. Finally they decided they could manage the resources to offer both the IB and the APS.

It was not until the end of the second year that they really came to grips with the design of the new Professional and Technical Program, to start implementation the following year. It turned out that the faculty and some of the employers had very different ideas about what the school curriculum should look like, how assessment should be done, and what the role of the employers should be.

Somehow, everything that had been settled before became unsettled. If the unexamined life is not worth living, then they were all leading very worthwhile professional lives. Anne and the rest of the faculty came, over time, to see that what they most needed was professional development, but not of the usual lecture sort. What they needed was a disciplined way to get the knowledge and skills they needed so they could reach the goals they had set for themselves. Some of that skill and knowledge came through reading everything they could in order to find out what districts and schools anywhere were doing the best job of tackling problems like those they had at Adams. When they had identified those who did it best, they would work at finding out how they did it, how they would, with hindsight, do it differently if they had to start again, and how the practices they had found might be changed to make them fit better with the situation at Adams High. Some of their professional development support came from the organizations that had developed the standards and assessments they were using. The state university worked closely with them as did a national organization that had come up with a high school design the faculty liked. What Anne and her colleagues saw clearly was that they had to make sure that all these sources of advice and ideas were working in harness, not at cross purposes. They were not isolated workshops, but in a sense, a way that external people could work with the faculty to help promote a continuing search for knowledge that was very focused on the common work at hand.

Though Anne would come home dog tired in those times, she began to realize after awhile that she was also totally reinvigorated, almost a new person. This whole effort had re-energized not only her but a very large fraction of the faculty. Everyone was learning at a furious rate. Long established ways of doing things that none of them had thought would ever be changed were falling by the wayside every day. Ancient antagonisms with other institutions in the community were being replaced by warm personal relationships and a can do spirit. It seemed that no matter how early Anne came into school and how late she left it, there were teachers there before she arrived and after she left, working on things alone and in groups that mattered very much to them. There was a certain electricity in the air.

Occasionally, Anne's mind would drift into the future. She knew the staff could not keep up this pace forever. The question was how they could begin to build habit tracks into the system they were building that would increase the odds that what they had built would outlast them, would become the established way that things were done at Adams. But then her mind would inevitably be drawn back to the present and her pleasure at what had been achieved.

By far the best part was what was happening to the students and their parents. There was new hope where there had been no hope before. The sullen response was giving way to quiet requests for help. The discipline problems began to melt away as students began to feel that someone among the adults believed in them, was interested in them and would actually help them. Students who had never had anything but trouble reading were now meeting the standard of reading 25 books a year and much more. Success was breeding success, instead of failure breeding failure as had been the case for so many for so long.

And the very symbol of everything that had gone right was mounting the stage right now.

"Congratulations, Debbie. I am so happy for you!"

"Oh, Mrs. Anderson, I cannot thank you enough for everything you and this school have done for me."

"Oh, Debbie, you already have, just by being on stage. Let us hear from you now, hear?"

And Anne watched Debbie stride across the stage, knowing that she had the best job in the world.

References

American Federation of Teachers. (1997). *Making standards matter: A fifty-state progress report on efforts to raise academic standards.* Washington, DC: Author.

Beaton, A. E., Martin, M. O., Mullis, I. V. S., Gonzalez, E. J., Smith, T. A. & Kelly, D. L. (1996a). *Mathematics achievement in the middle school years: IEA's third international mathematics and science study.* Chestnut Hill, MA: Boston College.

Beaton, A. E., Martin, M. O., Mullis, I. V. S., Gonzalez, E. J., Smith, T. A. & Kelly, D. L. (1996b). *Science achievement in the middle school years: IEA's third international mathematics and science study.* Chestnut Hill, MA: Boston College.

Beaton, A. E., Mullis, I. V. S., Martin, M. O., Gonzalez, E. J., Kelly, D. L., & Smith, T. A. (1997a). *Mathematics achievement in the primary school years: IEA's third international mathematics and science study.* Chestnut Hill, MA: Boston College.

Beaton, A. E., Mullis, I. V. S., Martin, M. O., Gonzalez, E. J., Kelly, D. L., & Smith, T. A. (1997b). *Science achievement in the primary school years: IEA's third international mathematics and science study.* Chestnut Hill, MA: Boston College.

Business Task Force on Student Standards. (1995). *The challenge of change: Standards to make education work for all our children.* Washington, DC: Business Coalition for Education Reform

Caldwell, B. J., & Hayward, D. K. (1998). *The future of schools: Lessons from the reform of public education.* London: Falmer.

Callahan, R. (1962). *Education and the cult of efficiency.* Chicago: University of Chicago Press.

Carroll, L. (1832). *Alice in wonderland.* New York: Norton.

Commission on the Skills of the American Workforce. (1990). *America's Choice: high skills or low wages!* Rochester, NY: National Center on Education and the Economy.

Conant, J. B. (1959). *The American high school today.* New York: McGraw-Hill.

Conant, J. B. (1967). *The comprehensive high school: A second report to interested citizens.* New York: McGraw-Hill.

Cremin, L. (1964). *The transformation of the school: Progressivism in American education 1876-1957.* New York: Knopf.

Darling-Hammond, L. (1997). *The right to learn: A blueprint for creating schools that work.* San Francisco: Jossey-Bass.

Department of Education, National Center for Education Statistics. (1996). *The condition of education, 1996.* Washington, DC: Government Printing Office.

Dewey, J. (1899). *The school and society.* Chicago: University of Chicago Press.

Fullan, M. (1993). *Change forces: Probing the depths of educational reform.* London: Falmer.

Golding, W. (1911). *Lord of the flies.* London: Faber & Faber.

Hargraves, A., Earl, L. & Ryan, J. (1996). *Schooling for change: Reinventing education for early adolescents.* London: Falmer.

Hofstadter, R. (1963). *Anti-intellectualism in American life.* New York: Knopf.

Johnson, J., & Farkas, S. (1997). *Getting by: What American teenagers really think about their schools.* New York: Public Agenda.

Kennedy, J. F. (1956). *Profiles in courage.* New York: Harper.

Kentucky Department of Education. (1995). *Kentucky education reform: The first five years 1990-1995.* Frankfort, KY: Department of Education Publications Center.

Knowles, J. (1990). *A separate peace.* Boston: Twayne. (Original work published 1926)

Lawler, E. E. (1996). *From the ground up: Six principles for building the new logic corporation.* San Francisco: Jossey-Bass.

Lieberman, A., & Grolnick, M. (1997). Networks, reform and the professional development of teachers. In A. Hargraves (Ed.), *1997 ASCD yearbook: Rethinking educational change with heart and mind* (pp. 192-215). Alexandria, VA: Association for Supervision and Curriculum Development.

Lieberman, A., & McLaughlin, M. (1992). Networks for educational change: Powerful and problematic. *Phi Delta Kappan, 73*(9), 673-677.

Little, J. W. (1993). Teachers' professional development in a climate of educational reform. *Educational Evaluation and Policy Analysis, 5*(2), 129-151.

Marsh, D. D. (1996). Making school reform work: Lessons from successful schools. *Thrust for Educational Leadership, 26*(3), 10-14.

Marsh, D. D. (1995). *Restructuring for results: High performance management in the Edmonton public schools.* Washington, DC: National Center on Education and the Economy.

Marsh, D. D., & Crocker, P. S. (1991). School restructuring: Implementing middle school reform. In A. R. Odden (Ed.), *Educational policy implementation* (pp. 259-278). Albany: State University of New York Press.

Marshall, R., & Tucker, M. (1992). *Thinking for a living: Education and the wealth of nations.* New York: Basic Books.

McDonald, J. P. (1996). *Redesigning school: Lessons for the 21st century.* San Francisco: Jossey-Bass.

Meier, D. W. (1995). *The power of their ideas: Lessons for America from a small school in Harlem.* Boston: Beacon.

Muncey, D. E., & McQuillan, P. J. (1996). *Reform and resistance in schools and classrooms.* New Haven, CT: Yale University Press.

National Center on Education and the Economy. (1997). *Planning for results.* Washington, DC: Author.

National Council of Teachers of Mathematics. (1989). *Curriculum and evaluation standards for school mathematics.* Reston, VA: Author.

National Education Goals Panel, Technical Planning Group. (1993). *Promises to keep: Creating high standards for American students.* Washington, DC: Author.

Newmann, F. M., & Associates (1996). *Authentic achievement: Restructuring schools for intellectual quality.* San Francisco: Jossey-Bass.

New Standards. (1997). *Performance standards* (Vol. 1: Elementary school, Vol. 2: Middle school, Vol. 3: High school). Washington, DC: National Center on Education and the Economy.

Peak, L. (1996). *Pursuing excellence.* Washington, DC: Government Printing Office.

Powell, A. G., Farrar, E., & Cohen, D. K. (1985). *The shopping mall high school: Winners and losers in the educational marketplace.* Boston: Houghton Mifflin.

Rothman, R. (1995). *Measuring up: Standards, assessment, and school reform.* San Francisco: Jossey-Bass.

Rothman, R. (1997). *How to make the link between standards, assessment, and real student achievement.* Arlington, VA: New American Schools.

Schlechty, P. (1997). *Inventing better schools: An action plan for educational reform.* San Francisco: Jossey-Bass.

Schmidt, W. H., et al. (1996). *Characterizing pedagogical flow.* Dordrecht, The Netherlands: Kluwer.

Schmidt, W. H., McKnight, C. C., & Raizen, S. A. (1997). *A splintered vision: An investigation of U.S. science and mathematics education.* Dordrecht, The Netherlands: Kluwer.

Sillitoe, A. (1959). *The loneliness of the long-distance runner.* New York: Knopf.

Sizer, T. R. (1985). *Horace's compromise: The dilemma of the American high school.* Boston: Houghton Mifflin.

Sizer, T. R. (1992). *Horace's school: Redesigning the American high school.* Boston: Houghton Mifflin.

Sizer, T. R. (1996). *Horace's hope: What works for the American high school.* Boston: Houghton Mifflin.

Sparks, D., & Hirsh, S. (1997). *A new vision for staff development.* Alexandria, VA: Association for Supervision and Curriculum Development.

Stigler, J. W., & Hiebert, J. (1997). Understanding and improving classroom mathematics instruction. *Phi Delta Kappan, 79*(1), 14-21.

Tucker, M., & Codding, J. (1995). *Organizing alliance schools for results.* Washington, DC: National Center on Education and the Economy.

Tucker, M., & Codding, J. (1998). *Standards for our schools: How to set them, measure them, and reach them.* San Francisco: Jossey-Bass.

Tyack, D. (1974). *The one best system: A history of American urban education.* Cambridge, MA: Harvard University Press.

Wasley, P. A., Hampel, R. L., & Clark, R. W. (1997). *Kids and school reform.* San Francisco: Jossey-Bass.

Webster's seventh new collegiate dictionary. (1963). Springfield, MA: Merriam Company.

Wiggins, G. (1993). *Assessing student performance.* San Francisco: Jossey-Bass.

Selected Bibliography

Advanced Placement Program, College Board. (1994). *National summary reports.* Princeton, NJ: College Entrance Examination Board and Educational Testing.

Archbald, D. A., & Newmann F. M. (1988). *Beyond standardized testing: Assessing authentic academic achievement in the secondary school.* Reston, VA: National Association of Secondary School Principals.

Bishop, J. (1990). *Incentives for learning: Why American high school students compare so poorly to their counterparts overseas.* Ithaca, NY: Cornell University.

Boyer, E. L., & the Carnegie Foundation for the Advancement of Teaching. (1983). *High school: A report on secondary education in America.* New York: Harper & Row.

Caldwell, B. J. (1996). *Beyond the self-managing school.* Keynote address at the annual conference of the British Educational Management and Administration Society, Coventry, UK.

Caldwell, B. J., & Spinks, J. (1992). *Leading the self-managing school.* London: Falmer.

California Department of Education. (1987). *Caught in the middle: Educational reform for young adolescents in California public schools.* Sacramento: Author.

California High School Task Force. (1992). *Second to none: A vision of the new California high school.* Sacramento: California Department of Education.

Carnegie Council on Adolescent Development. (1995). *Great transitions: Preparing adolescents for a new century.* New York: Author.

Carnegie Foundation for the Advancement of Teaching. (1988). *An imperiled generation: Saving urban schools.* Princeton, NJ: Princeton University Press.

Carnegie Task Force on the Education of Young Adolescents. (1989). *Turning points: Preparing American youth for the 21st century.* Washington, DC: Carnegie Council on Adolescent Development.

Coleman, J. (1988). *High school and beyond: A national longitudinal study for the 1980's.* Washington, DC: National Center for Educational Statistics.

Coleman, J. S., & Hoffer, T. (1926). *Public and private high schools: The impact of communities.* New York: Basic Books.

College Board. (1996). *High school code: SAT program.* Princeton, NJ: College Entrance Examination Board and Educational Testing.

Commission on the Skills of the American Workforce. (1990). *America's Choice: high skills or low wages!* Rochester, NY: National Center on Education and the Economy.

Davies, B., & Ellison, L. (Eds.) (1994). *Managing the effective primary school.* London: Longman.

Deal, T., & Kennedy, A. A. (1982). *Corporate cultures: The rites and rituals of corporate life.* Reading, MA: Addison-Wesley.

Edelman, P. B., & Ladner, J. (Eds.). (1991). *Adolescence and poverty: Challenge for the 1990s.* Washington, DC: Center for National Policy Press.

Educational Testing Service. (1996). *Report in brief: NAEP 1994 trends in academic progress.* Washington, DC: Department of Education.

Elmore, R. F. et al. (1990). *Restructuring schools: The next generation of educational reform.* San Francisco: Jossey-Bass.

Gardner, H. (1991). *The unschooled mind: How children think and how schools should teach.* New York: Basic Books.

Goodlad, J. I. (in press). *A place called school.* New York: McGraw-Hill.

Gurr, D. (1995). *The leadership role of principals in selected "secondary schools of the future": Principal and teacher perspectives.* Unpublished EdD thesis, University of Melbourne, Melbourne, Australia.

Hallinger, P., Leithwood, K., & Murphy, J. (Eds.). (1993). *Cognitive perspectives on educational leadership.* New York: Teachers College Press.

Hampel, R. L. (1986). *The last little citadel: American high schools since 1940.* Boston: Houghton Mifflin.

Holmes, G., & Davies, B. (1994). Strategic management in primary schools. In B. Davies & L. Ellison (Eds.), *Managing the effective primary school* (pp. 16-33). London: Longman.

Johnston, W. B., & Packer, A. H. (1987). *Workforce 2000: Work and workers for the 21st century.* Indianapolis, IN: Hudson Institute.

Kearns, D. T., & Doyle, D. P. (1989). *Winning the brain race: A bold plan to make our school competitive.* San Francisco: ICS.

Kouzes, J., & Posner, B. (1995). *The leadership challenge: How to keep getting extraordinary things done in organizations.* San Francisco: Jossey-Bass.

Kozol, J. (1992). *Savage inequalities: Children in America's schools.* New York: Trumpet.

Lambert, L., Walker, D., Zimmerman, D., Cooper, J., Lambert, M. D., Gardner, M., & Slack, P. J. (1995). *The constructivist leader.* New York: Teachers College Press.

Lawler, E. E. (1992). *The ultimate advantage: Creating the high involvement organization.* San Francisco: Jossey-Bass.

Leithwood, K., & Steinbach, R. (1995). *Expert problem solving: Evidence from school and district leaders.* Albany: State University of New York Press.

Lewis, A. (1989). *Restructuring America's schools.* Arlington, VA: American Association of School Administrators.

Lightfoot, S. L. (1985). *Good high school portraits of character and culture.* New York: Basic Books.

Louis, K. S., & Miles, M. B. (1990). *Improving the urban high school: What works and why.* New York: Teachers College Press.

Marsh, D. D. (1992). Enhancing instructional leadership: Lessons from the California school leadership academy. *Education and Urban Society, 24*(3), 386-409.

Marsh, D. D. (1996). Making school reform work: Lessons from successful schools. *Thrust for Educational Leadership, 26*(3), 10-14.

Mehlinger, H. D. (1995). *School reform in the information age.* Bloomington, IN: Center for Excellence in Education.

Mohrman, S. (1994). Making the transition to high-performance management. In S. Mohrman, P. Wohlstetter, & Associates (Eds.), *School-based management: Organizing for high performance* (pp. 323-348). San Francisco: Jossey-Bass.

Mohrman, S., Wohlstetter, P., & Associates. (1994). *School-based management: Organizing for high performance.* San Francisco: Jossey-Bass.

Murnane, R. & Levy, F. (1996). *Teaching the new basic skills: Principles for educating children to thrive in a changing economy.* New York: Free Press.

Murphy, J. (1990). Principal instructional leadership. *Advances in Educational Administration: Changing Perspectives on the School, 1,* 163-200.

Murphy, J. (1994). Transformational change and the evolving role of the principal: Early empirical evidence. In J. Murphy & K. S. Louis (Eds.), *Reshaping the principalship: Insights from transformational reform efforts* (pp. 20-53). Thousand Oaks, CA: Corwin.

Murphy, J., & Louis, K. S. (Eds.). (1994). *Reshaping the principalship: Insights from transformational reform efforts.* Thousand Oaks, CA: Corwin.

National Center for Research in Vocational Education. (1990). *The cunning hand, the cultured mind: Models for integrating vocational and academic education.* Berkeley: University of California Press.

National Commission on Excellence in Education. (1990). *A nation at risk: The imperative for educational reform.* Washington, DC: Department of Education.

Newmann, F. M. (1991). Can depth replace coverage in the high school curriculum. *Phi Delta Kappan, 69,* 345-348.

Newmann, F. M. (1991). *Final report, National Center on Effective Secondary Schools.* Madison, WI: Wisconsin Center for Education Research.

Oakes, J. (1986). *Keeping track: How schools structure inequality.* New Haven, CT: Yale University Press.

Oakes, J. (1991). *Alternatives to tracking: Are there critical commonplaces?* Chicago: American Educational Research Association.

Oakes, J., & Lipton, M. (1990). *Making the best of schools: A handbook for parents, teachers and policy makers.* New Haven, CT: Yale University Press.

Odden, A. R. (1995). *Educational leadership for America's schools.* New York: McGraw-Hill.

Organization for Economic Co-operation and Development. (1995). *Performance standards in education: In search of quality.* Paris: OECD Publications.

O'Toole, J. (1995). *Leading change: Overcoming the ideology of comfort and the tyranny of custom.* San Francisco: Jossey-Bass.

Public Agenda. (1997). *Getting by: What American teenagers really think about their schools.* New York: Author.

Ravitch, D. (1995). *National standards in American education: A citizen's guide.* Washington, DC: Brookings Institution.

Schmidt, W. H., et al. (1996). *Characterizing pedagogical flow.* Dordrecht, The Netherlands: Kluwer.

Secretary's Commission on Achieving Necessary Skills. (1991). *What work requires of schools: A SCANS report for America 2000.* Washington, DC: Department of Labor.

Sedlak, M. W., Wheeler, C. W., Pullin, D. C., & Cusick, P. A. (1986). *Selling students short: Classroom bargains and academic reform in the American high school.* New York: Teachers College Press.

Senge, P. (1990). *The fifth discipline: The art and practice of the learning organization.* London: Doubleday.

Sergiovanni, T. J. (1990). *Value-added leadership.* New York: Harcourt Brace.

Smith, M. S., & O'Day, J. A. (1991). Systemic schools reform. In S. Fuhrman & B. Malen (Eds.), *The politics of curriculum and testing* (pp. 233-267). Bristol, PA: Falmer.

Steinberg, L. (1996). *Beyond the classroom: Why school reform has failed and what parents need to do.* New York: Simon & Schuster.

Stevenson, H., & Stigler, J. (1994). *The learning gap: Why our schools are failing and what we can learn from Japanese and Chinese education.* New York: Touchstone.

Tucker, M. (1994). *The certificate of initial mastery: A primer.* Washington, DC: National Center on Education and the Economy.

Tucker, M. (1994). *The international experience with school leaving examinations.* Washington, DC: National Center on Education and the Economy.

Tucker, M. (1994). *States begin developing the certificate of initial mastery.* Washington, DC: National Center on Education and the Economy.

Tucker, M., & Codding, J. (1998). *Standards for our schools: How to set them, measure them, and reach them.* San Francisco: Jossey-Bass.

Tyack, D., & Cuban, L. (1995). *Tinkering towards utopia.* Cambridge, MA: Harvard University Press.

U.S. Department of Education. (1991). *America 2000: An education strategy.* Washington, DC: Author.

Index